THE VANCOUVER SUN's
BEST PLANT PICKS

Your Month-by-Month Guide for a West Coast Garden

STEVE WHYSALL

whitecap

Edited by Taryn Boyd
Proofread by Grace Yaginuma
Design by Janine Vangool
Photography credits listed on page 256

Printed in Canada by Friesens.

Library and Archives Canada Cataloguing in Publication

Whysall, Steve, 1950–
    The Vancouver sun's best plant picks : your month-by-month guide for
a West Coast garden / Steve Whysall.

Includes index.
ISBN 978-1-55285-927-8

    1. Gardening—British Columbia—Pacific Coast. 2. Plants,
Ornamental—British Columbia—Pacific Coast. I. Title. II. Title: Best
plant picks.

SB453.3.C2W485 2008   635.909711'1   C2007-905172-3

The publisher acknowledges the financial support of the Government of
Canada through the Book Publishing Industry Development Program (BPIDP)
and the Province of British Columbia through the Book Publishing Tax Credit.

For Loraine

Contents

Introduction

This book is a month-by-month guide to the best plants to use in a coastal garden to achieve either flower or foliage interest throughout the year. That is, with a little foresight and planning, you can have a seamless procession of flowers and foliage in your garden—as one plant fades, another will rise to take its place.

Your garden can look fabulous all year round, even in January: look up *Daphne odora, Helleborus argutifolius, Sarcococca humilis* and *Viburnum tinus.* For flowers in April, try *Alchemilla mollis, Aquilegia vulgaris, Brunnera* 'Jack Frost' and *Rhododendron augustinii.* To brighten the darker days of November, there's *Aucuba japonica, Camellia sasanqua* and *Skimmia japonica.*

How to use this book

Best Plant Picks is organized quite simply in a month-by-month sequence, featuring plants that either have great flowers, excellent foliage or attractive structure (or all three) during any given month. You can use this book in a variety of ways:

1. Look up a plant using the index, and read all about that particular plant's characteristics and how to make the best use of it in the garden.

2. See if your garden seems to be missing a beat at a certain time of year. Then consult the appropriate months to find plant suggestions to solve your problem.

3. Simply use this book to plan a new garden, selecting top performance plants from each month to guarantee that your finished work has something of interest in every month of the year.

Where it began

I began writing brief plant profiles in 1994 as a weekly mini-feature in the *Vancouver Sun*. It was originally called Plant of the Week and was intended as a concise profile of a plant in bloom.

The initial idea was to identify a particular plant, and go over the pros and cons of growing it, as well as explain where to plant it, how to take care of it, how to prune it (if necessary), how to propagate it and where it could be bought. It was meant to be a "quick read," but packed with useful information.

By 2001, the name of the column changed to Flowering Now. In 2005, the name changed again to In Flower. By then, it had become clear that readers were mainly interested in three key pieces of information: What does the plant have to offer in terms of great flowers or foliage (or, in other words, why should I have it in my garden)? How big does it grow? And, what conditions does it need to thrive?

All of this information was eventually distilled into an even more compact format consisting of a few simple paragraphs and a photograph of the plant. Few readers, it seemed, were interested in knowing how to propagate plants; they were perfectly happy to leave that often difficult task to professional growers.

In 2006, In Flower changed its name again to Plant Pick. The feature has since run every Friday on the front of the *Sun*'s At Home section.

Over the years, I have written hundreds of these short plant profiles. The same plant was sometimes featured more than once, although the information changed to focus on a different aspect of the plant's personality.

Throughout this process, *Sun* readers got an almost encyclopedic amount of information about plants during the course of the year. Many people began clipping these mini-profiles and compiling their own scrapbooks. I hope *The Vancouver Sun's Best Plant Picks* will give them a more complete, user-friendly and durable reference that will be useful for many years.

INTRO

What's in a name?

All the plants in this book are listed by both their correct botanical name and their common name(s). This is not to impress you with clever botanical nomenclature. It is simply to ensure that you get the right plant. For instance, if you were to wander into your local garden centre and ask for a viburnum, the first thing you would be asked is, "What kind of viburnum?" The problem is that there are more than two hundred species of viburnum. Unless you can say specifically which one you want, you are more than likely to come away with one you don't want.

You will find the same problem if you use only common names. For instance, if you ask for a pink geranium, the person at the garden centre will want to know whether you really want a geranium or if you mean a pelargonium (the correct name for what most people call "geraniums"). Or are you looking for a "hardy geranium" (a true geranium) and if so, which kind?

When it comes to botanical names, there are things you need to know, and things not worth worrying about. You need to know that each plant belongs to a specific group called a genus. This is indicated by the plant's first name. *Acer*, for example, is the genus name for maples. Think of it as a kind of surname. Now, within that group of maples there are many kinds, or species. Each plant has been given a second (species) name—for instance, *Acer griseum*, *Acer davidii* and *Acer palmatum*.

But if you went to the garden centre and asked for an *Acer palmatum*, they would then ask you, "What cultivar?" This is why plants often have a third name, which is the cultivar name. This appears in single quotation marks: *Acer palmatum* 'Bloodgood', for example. With this information, you can ask for precisely the plant you want and get it. You need all three names to be sure.

Botanical names get more complicated after this. Sometimes a plant has an extra Latinized name after the species names that indicates something about the plant's growth habit (for example, *fastigiata* means "erect" and *pendula* means "weeping"), colour (*alba*, "white"; *glauca*, "blue green"), flowers (*campanulata*, "bell shaped"; *stellata*, "star shaped") or geographical origin (*japonica*, "of Japan"; *sinensis*, "of China").

When a plant is a hybrid between two or more species, taxonomists use a multiplication sign to let you know. *Epimedium* × *rubrum*, for example, is a hybrid produced by crossing *Epimedium alpinum* with *Epimedium grandiflorum*.

Do you care? Probably not. Most home gardeners don't. If you go to your garden centre and ask for *Epimedium* × *rubrum* but neglect to include the multiplication sign, you will still come away with the right plant. However, for botanical accuracy, you will find plants in this book have been given their correct full botanical name and, in some cases, this includes an × sign.

Coastal gardens

There are few better places in the world to be a gardener than right here in the Pacific Northwest. This is not mere regional pride, it's a scientific fact. Those of us lucky enough to live on the West Coast can grow thousands of plants that gardeners in other parts of North America can only dream of having in their garden.

North America is mapped out into ten climate zones, based on average minimum winter temperatures. The lower the zone number, the colder it gets. The higher the zone number, the warmer it stays and the more plants can grow. Most of the Pacific Northwest falls into either Zone 7 (0 to 10°F/ –18 to –12°C) or Zone 8 (10 to 20°F/–12 to –7°C). There are colder inland areas where winter temperatures dip to –10 to –30°F (–23 to –35°C), and there are hot spots where temperatures rarely fall below freezing.

Zone numbers are a useful guide when buying plants. If the label on the plant indicates that it is hardy only in Zones 9 to 10, you can assume it is too tender to survive outdoors in most coastal gardens.

This doesn't tell the whole story. There are other climatic factors, such as rainfall and winds and freeze-thaw cycles, to take into consideration. This is often the reason why identical plants perform differently in neighbouring gardens: one is basking in the warmth of a microclimate with a higher zone rating, while the other is fighting for survival in poorly drained ground that keeps freezing and thawing.

Zone numbers are useful, but they should not stop you from experimenting with plants. Many plants brought to Europe from China were initially thought to be tender and were overwintered in heated greenhouses until someone had the nerve to try growing them outside and discovered that they were actually extremely hardy.

JANUARY

→ NOTES

TO-DO LIST

- ○ Browse seed catalogues and place an order, or pick up seed at your local garden centre.
- ○ Start planning your vegetable garden and decide which vegetables and herbs to grow.
- ○ Start seed indoors for summer flowers.
- ○ Weather permitting, dig over existing flower beds or prepare new ones.
- ○ Keep bulbs in containers lightly watered to maintain proper development.
- ○ Check that dahlia tubers are not drying out, and keep an eye on overwintered fuchsias and pelargoniums for whitefly and signs of rot.
- ○ Knock heavy snowfall from bushes, hedges and evergreens to prevent branch damage.
- ○ Prune fruit trees and late-flowering deciduous shrubs. Snip back lateral and side branches of wisteria to within two or three buds.
- ○ Spray fruit trees and roses with dormant oil and lime sulphur. Do this when the plants have no leaves to kill overwintering insects and diseases.
- ○ Bring birds to the garden by putting out a feeder or hanging a seed bell where birds can see it.
- ○ Visit your garden centre to find hellebores, as well as deals on last year's containers.
- ○ Enjoy the heavenly fragrance of witch hazel.

JANUARY

Acer palmatum 'Sango kaku'

CORAL BARK MAPLE

→ This spectacular little tree is especially noticeable in the winter garden because of its beautiful bright reddish-coral bark and branches. The Japanese name 'Sango kaku' means "coral tower" or "coral pillar," but the tree was once known as 'Senkak', a name you may still find on some plant labels.

'Sango kaku' offers three seasons of interest. It has delicate, pale pinkish-green leaves in summer, which turn into striking canary-yellow, gold and apricot foliage in the fall. And there is the beautiful coral-coloured bark, which is intensified by cold weather, turning more salmon pink in winter.

The tree has also been awarded the Royal Horticultural Society's prestigious Award of Garden Merit.

TYPE *tree*

SIZE *15 feet (4.5 m)*

LOCATION *part shade*

CONDITIONS *acidic, well-drained soil*

Daphne odora

WINTER DAPHNE

→ Daphne is said to possess the world's most powerful fragrance. And winter-flowering *Daphne odora* is thought to be the most fragrant of them all. Its blooms have been described as having the fragrance of an ambrosia dessert with hints of orange and coconut. It has dense clusters of star-shaped, purple-pink flowers.

Grow your daphne close to a doorway or entrance or beside paths where the sweet scent can best be appreciated. You may also want to clip a few branches to bring indoors. The fragrance can fill a room.

D. odora 'Aureomarginata' is a little more cold resistant, less prone to viral disease and has equally fragrant flowers. However, it has variegated green leaves with creamy yellow edges, which is something not all gardeners find attractive.

TYPE *shrub*

SIZE *4 feet (1.2 m)*

LOCATION *full sun to part shade*

CONDITIONS *moist but well-drained soil*

TYPE
shrub

SIZE
*10 to 16 feet
(3 to 5 m)*

LOCATION
full sun to part shade

CONDITIONS
*moist but well-
drained soil*

Hamamelis √

WITCH HAZEL

→ In the dark days of winter, colour in the garden can lift our spirit. It reminds us that spring is only weeks away. It is always worthwhile to clip a few branches of this exquisite winter-flowering shrub to bring indoors where you can more fully enjoy the fragrant spidery yellow or bronze-red flowers. If buds have not yet fully opened, a branch can be forced into bloom by placing it in a warm room.

Witch hazel gets its name from the use of the twigs as "witching sticks," or divining rods to dowse for water. Its fragrance and flowers are magical, appearing in the depths of winter when nothing else is in bloom. As well as its great scent, witch hazel has striking fall foliage with leaves that turn orange or scarlet in October. The leaves and bark can be used to make a healing astringent.

Favourite cultivars of witch hazel are mostly forms of *Hamamelis × intermedia*, a cross between *H. japonica* and *H. mollis*, and includes 'Jelena' (coppery orange), 'Arnold's Promise' (deep yellow), 'Diane' (red), 'Pallida' (sulphur yellow) and 'Ruby Glow' (coppery red). The yellow varieties tend to have the best fragrance.

The Royal Horticultural Society recommends annual feeding with fertilizer, as well as mulching and extra watering in dry spells. Apparently, all of this not only promotes strong growth but discourages suckering.

Chinese witch hazel (*H. mollis*) is also worth checking out. It is a large spreading shrub or small tree with dependable golden-yellow blooms.

Japanese maples, enkianthus, euonymous and winter-flowering heathers all make good companions.

JANUARY

Helleborus argutifolius

CORSICAN HELLEBORE

TYPE
perennial

SIZE
*3 to 4 feet
(90 cm to 1.2 m)*

LOCATION
light shade

CONDITIONS
fertile, well-drained soil

→ With its thick, leathery leaves with serrated edges, the Corsican hellebore is a wonderfully architectural plant for the winter garden. It produces lime-green flowers in early spring.

It prefers light shade, but tolerates some sun and especially benefits from all the light it can get in winter. In some spots it needs to be staked to stop it from flopping over, particularly if hit by heavy snow.

Flowers start to appear in January and continue blooming to April when they need to be snipped off, along with the old foliage, to make way for all the emerging new growth.

Top cultivars are 'Silver Lace' with silvery-pewter foliage, 'Pacific Frost' with speckled foliage and 'Little Ebert', a dwarf cultivar that grows only 15 inches (38 cm) high.

Also check out *Helleborus × sternii* (a cross between *H. argutifolius* and *H. lividus),* which has dark greyish green leaves and chartreuse flowers. It grows 12 to 24 inches (30 to 60 cm) high. Like *H. argutifolius,* these also flourish in a location that gets more sun than shade.

Mahonia × media 'Charity'

OREGON GRAPE

→ One of the most striking evergreen shrubs in the winter garden, this has distinctive dark green holly-like leaves and dramatic sprays of fragrant yellow flowers that can last from December to April. Flowers are followed by clusters of blue-black berries in late summer. It is these berries that give mahonia its common name Oregon grape.

'Charity', a cultivar developed in Northern Ireland in 1950, can reach 10 to 15 feet (3 to 4.5 m) if not pruned, but with routine trimming it can be kept down to 4 to 5 feet (1.2 to 1.5 m).

All mahonias are mostly grown for their attractive foliage and fragrant, showy yellow flowers. 'Charity' has a more upright habit, giving it a strong structural form.

Other popular cultivars include 'Lionel Fortescue', 'Winter Sun' and 'Arthur Menzies'. Seed-grown offsprings of 'Charity' are 'Faith' and 'Hope', which have soft-yellow flowers. Neither is as good as its parent.

Mahonia aquifolium is native to the woodlands of the Pacific Northwest and grows 6 to 10 feet (1.8 to 3 m) high. 'Compacta' and 'Mayhan Strain' are smaller, growing only 3 to 4 feet (90 cm to 1.2 m), while 'Apollo' is a dwarf cultivar, ideal for growing under trees or as a ground cover. (What is even more ideal as a ground cover, however, are varieties of *M. repens*.)

TYPE
shrub

SIZE
*10 to 15 feet
(3 to 4.5 m)*

LOCATION
part shade to full sun

CONDITIONS
moist but well-drained soil

JANUARY

Picea pungens

COLORADO BLUE SPRUCE

TYPE
conifer

SIZE
*40 to 50 feet
(12 to 15 m)*

LOCATION
Full sun to part shade

CONDITIONS
*moist but well-
drained soil*

→ The Colorado blue spruce is outstanding in January, especially when contrasted against a blanket of snow or with a layer of frost on its bright, steel-blue needles.

There are many different cultivars from which to choose, but Hoop's blue spruce (*Picea pungens* 'Hoopsii') is the bluest with stiff horizontal branches densely covered in silvery-blue needles.

Relatively slow-growing, it grows 8 feet (2.5 m) high after ten years. Its growth can be somewhat irregular for the first few years, but the bright silver-blue needles are spectacular and easily make up for any perceived flaws.

Other notable cultivars of *P. pungens* are 'Fat Albert', 'Moerheim', 'Koster' and 'Thomsen'. First-class dwarf blue spruces include 'Globosa', 'Glauca Compacta' and 'Papoose'.

For a low-growing variety to tuck under maple trees there's 'Prostrata' or 'Glauca Procumbens', both of which are ground-hugging and slow-growing.

Primula acaulis

PRIMROSE

→ You know spring isn't far away when you see thousands of pots of brightly coloured *Primula acaulis* popping up at your neighbourhood garden centre, corner store or supermarket.

Tens of thousands of these primulas are commercially produced for the late-winter market. Growers recognize that they are indeed a welcome foretaste of spring. You'll find them in a wide range of colours from white, yellow and orange to purple, pink and red.

The Danova series is most likely what you will find offered at your local store. Other key series include Supra, Unistar, Gala, Quantum, Tempra and Lira.

These flowers bring a cheeerful splash of colour to a container or window box, but being greenhouse-grown hybrids they are not very resilient and often don't survive for long when planted in the open garden.

Nevertheless, they brighten what otherwise is a pretty dreary month, and they can satisfy the gardener's longing to get planting.

TYPE
perennial

SIZE
4 inches (10 cm)

LOCATION
light shade

CONDITIONS
moist but well-drained soil

JANUARY

Prunus serrula

TIBETAN CHERRY

TYPE
tree

SIZE
30 feet (9 m)

LOCATION
full sun to part shade

CONDITIONS
moist but well-drained soil

→ The paperbark cherry is special because it has an exceptionally beautiful and shiny mahogany-coloured, peeling bark. This looks lovely in the winter garden when the colour is more noticeable due to the absence of competition.

In spring the tree has white flowers, followed by dark green leaves that turn yellow or red in autumn. It won an Award of Garden Merit from the Royal Horticultural Society.

The Tibetan cherry requires minimal pruning, usually to remove dead or dying branches in order to maintain the overall health of the tree. If pruning is needed, it should be done in late winter or early spring. As the tree ages, the trunk and branches tend to develop a gnarled appearance, but they never lose the beauty of their glossy, copper-brown bark.

If you like trees with beautiful bark you will also want to check out the paperbark maple (*Acer griseum*, page 25) and the white-barked birch (*Betula jacquemontii*, page 242), both of which are much admired for the exceptional colour and texture of their branches and trunks. Each one grows 25 to 30 feet (7.5 to 9 m) high.

Sarcococca ruscifolia

FRAGRANT SWEETBOX

→ You are most likely to discover this wonderful evergreen shrub when you are taken by surprise by its delicious perfume. The slight pungent vanilla fragrance of the creamy white flowers can stop you in your tracks as you pass by. It is always arresting, especially when sarcococca is mass-planted as a hedge.

In addition to a powerful and impressive fragrance, this shrub has two other outstanding qualities: it is evergreen, making it a quality plant for adding year-round structure and definition to the garden; and, unlike many plants, it is perfectly happy in the shade, and even thrives and flowers in deep shade.

There are two main species: Himalayan or Christmas box sarcococca (*Sarcococca hookeriana* var. *humilis*) and common sarcococca (*S. ruscifolia*).

Both are fragrant, but *S. ruscifolia* grows bigger with blood-red berries that ripen to reddish black after flowering. *S. humilis* is more compact, growing only 12 to 24 inches (30 to 60 cm), and it produces tiny and shiny purple-black berries after flowering.

TYPE
shrub

SIZE
*3 to 5 feet
(90 cm to 1.5 m)*

LOCATION
dappled shade

CONDITIONS
average, well-drained soil

JANUARY

Trachycarpus fortunei

WINDMILL PALM

TYPE
tree

SIZE
15 to 25 feet
(4.5 to 7.5 m)

LOCATION
full sun to part shade

CONDITIONS
fertile, well-drained soil

→ The windmill palm is a staple of the subtropical garden because of its beautiful, fan-shaped leaves and attractive trunk, which becomes covered with matted, hairlike fibre as the tree matures.

Its hardiness makes it appealing to coastal gardeners looking for a palm to give their gardens the look of the tropics. Native to Japan and China, the windmill palm is capable of tolerating several degrees of frost. It is also completely indifferent to rain and even thrives in beach locations where it is exposed to salty sea air.

Growing about 12 inches (30 cm) a year, it will reach its full height after ten years. Under ideal conditions, it can soar 30 to 50 feet (9 to 15 m).

In summer, the windmill palm produces clusters of yellow flowers on short stems that are tucked among the leaves, followed by dark blue seed heads that germinate fairly easily to produce new plants.

You will find this palm also listed as the "Chusan palm" or "hemp palm" and sometimes given a different botanical name, *Chamaerops excelsa*. Some BC municipalities have allowed it to be widely planted in high-profile areas such as next to beaches and along street medians.

Viburnum tinus

LAURUSTINUS

→ A beautiful and versatile evergreen shrub, *Viburnum tinus* has dainty clusters of fragrant white flowers from late winter to early spring. Flower buds are pink before they open white.

It can be either grown as a shrub in the mixed border or used to create an informal hedge. It can also be grown successfully in a container to add colour, fragrance and interest to an entrance in winter. It is better known in Europe as laurustinus, where it has been a firm garden favourite for four hundred years.

'Spring Bouquet' is one of the best cultivars. After flowering, it produces attractive clusters of metallic-blue berries that slowly turn black. Other top cultivars are 'Compactum', 'Variegatum', 'Lucidum', 'Eve Price' and 'Bewley's Variegated'.

In the right location, it is capable of flowering from November to April. It prefers soil that is evenly moist and has been enriched with organic matter. It will not do well if planted in dry shade.

Most gardens have room for more than one species of viburnum. Also check out *V. opulus* 'Sterile' (European snowball), *V. macrocephalum* (Chinese snowball), *V. plicatum* (Japanese snowball), *V. carlesii* 'Cayuga' (Korean spice viburnum), *V. plicatum tomentosum* 'Mariesii' and *V. plicatum* var. *tomentosum* 'Summer Snowflake' (one of the best summer-flowering shrubs for the garden).

TYPE
shrub

SIZE
6 to 10 feet
(1.8 to 3 m)

LOCATION
full sun to part shade

CONDITIONS
moist but well-drained soil

JANUARY

FEBRUARY

TO-DO LIST

○ *Remove weeds while they are clearly visible and check for slugs and snails at the same time.*

○ *Start to clean up the perennial border and flower beds by cutting back old stems, and bagging and disposing of leaves and other winter debris.*

○ *Cut back raspberry canes and other fruit bushes and plant new ones.*

○ *Prune deciduous trees.*

- ○ Prune Buddleia davidii *(butterfly bush) and other summer-flowering shrubs like* Fuchsia magellanica *(hardy fuchsia) as well as C-type clematis that bloom after June. (However, do not prune spring-flowering shrubs until after they have bloomed.)*
- ○ *Prune back both campsis (trumpet vine) and the side-shoots of wisteria to within two or three buds.*
- ○ *Sow hardy annuals (such as bachelor buttons, sweet peas and California poppies) outdoors.*
- ○ *Start tender and half-hardy annuals such as cosmos, snapdragons, nicotiana, petunia, zinnia and salvia indoors.*
- ○ *Plant peas and broad beans. Radishes can be sown under cover; celery can be started indoors.*
- ○ *Weather permitting, plant trees, shrubs, lily bulbs, hellebores and bare-root roses.*
- ○ *On a mild day, spray roses, fruit trees and some shrubs with dormant oil.*
- ○ *Clean and sharpen tools. Get your lawn mower tuned up.*
- ○ *Remove moss and thatch from lawns by raking.*
- ○ *Lime lawns to counteract acidity and to achieve a desirable pH balance.*
- ○ *Enjoy the exquisite white flowers of Christmas rose* (Helleborus niger) *and the spidery yellow and copper-red flowers of witch hazel.*
- ○ *Discover the delightful sweet fragrance of the white flowers of sarcococca.*

FEBRUARY

Abeliophyllum distichum

WHITE FORSYTHIA

TYPE
shrub

SIZE
5 to 6 feet
(1.5 to 1.8 m)

LOCATION
full sun to light shade

CONDITIONS
average, well-drained soil

→ This plant might be hard to find at your local garden centre, but you will no doubt want to buy it immediately after you smell its super-fragrant star-shaped white flowers.

Native to central Korea, it is a deciduous shrub that flowers in mid- to late winter. The reason it is not more popular is that it doesn't do much the rest of the year.

Nevertheless, if you have space in your garden to indulge yourself with a few rare and unusual plants, this could be one of them. It would make a lovely addition and offers unusual winter interest.

It thrives in a protected south- or west-facing location where the plant gets shade in the afternoon during summer. Flowers can be damaged in very cold winters. Prune immediately after flowering.

Acer griseum

PAPERBARK MAPLE

→ Several outstanding trees capture our attention in winter. For example, the coral bark maple (*Acer palmatum* 'Sango kaku') has beautiful coral-red branches (page 12). The Tibetan cherry (*Prunus serrula*) has a polished mahogany-like trunk (page 18). The Himalayan birch (*Betula utilis jacquemontii*) has a dazzling pure white trunk (page 242). And *Stewartia monadelpha* (orangebark stewartia) has a lovely chestnut-brown trunk and branches.

But the paperbark maple (*Acer griseum*) is unique because of its fabulous peeling cinnamon-brown bark. It is a slow-growing tree native to central China, and looks best in a location where it receives morning or early evening sun.

It is never happy if left to struggle in dry ground, so it is wise to occasionally water it deeply through the summer. An excellent choice for gardens of all sizes, it has been given the Royal Horticultural Society's special Award of Garden Merit.

TYPE
tree

SIZE
*25 to 30 feet
(7.5 to 9 m)*

LOCATION
full sun to part shade

CONDITIONS
average, well-drained soil

FEBRUARY

TYPE
vine

SIZE
15 to 25 feet
(1.5 to 7.5 m)

LOCATION
full sun to light shade

CONDITIONS
average, well-drained soil

Clematis armandii

EVERGREEN CLEMATIS

→ Loved for its fabulous white, fragrant flowers and early spring blooming, *Clematis armandii* has the added value of having glossy green leaves all year round.

It is somewhat tender, so if planted in a cool north- or east-facing spot where it is exposed to frost and cold winds, it won't survive. But in a protected, sunny south- or west-facing location, where the roots are slightly shaded, it will flourish.

A vigorous grower, it will attach itself to all kinds of surfaces with tiny, twisty stems. It has been used to successfully drape fences, cover arbours and gazebos, as well as to dress up porches and patios.

Old leaves need to be cleaned away in spring, and the vine can be pruned after flowering. Do not prune back into old wood. Cut tips back only as far as there is healthy growth.

Top cultivars are 'Snowdrift' and 'Apple Blossom'. Other popular early spring-blooming clematis include varieties of *C. alpina* such as 'Jacqueline du Pre' (rosy mauve), 'Helsingborg' (deep purple), 'Pamela Jackman' (deep blue), 'Pink Flamingo' (pale pink) and 'Constance' (bright pink), all of which grow 8 to 12 feet (2.5 to 3.5 m), and cultivars of *C. macropetala* such as 'Blue Bird' (lavender blue), 'Jan Lindmark' (bluish pink), 'Markhams Pink' (light pink) and 'Rosie O'Grady' (light pink), all of which grow 8 to 10 feet (2.5 to 3 m).

FEBRUARY

Cornus mas

CORNELIAN CHERRY

→ Native to southern Europe, *Cornus mas* is technically a dogwood. This tree produces clusters of tiny yellow flowers on bare branches from the end of February into March. It also has a high resistance to pests, disease and air pollution, which makes it a good street tree for urban areas.

It gets its common name from the bright red fruit it bears in midsummer. Although the fruit is acidic, it is nonetheless edible and can be used to make jams and jellies. Unfortunately, the fruit is often quickly consumed by birds or squirrels or hidden by the tree's dark green leaves, so sometimes you don't see the fruit at all.

Its flaking bark makes it an interesting and appealing addition to the winter garden, but the pretty yellow flowers are the main reason most people bother to find a spot for it.

'Golden Glory' is the top cultivar. 'Redstone' has the best fruit production. Other rated cultivars include 'Jolico', 'Flava', 'Pioneer', 'Macrocarpa' and 'Variegata'. 'Nana' is a dwarf form.

TYPE
tree

SIZE
15 feet (4.5 m)

LOCATION
full sun to part shade

CONDITIONS
moist but well-drained soil

FEBRUARY

Corylopsis pauciflora

BUTTERCUP WINTER HAZEL

TYPE
shrub

SIZE
*6 to 8 feet
(1.8 to 2.5 m)*

LOCATION
part shade

CONDITIONS
moist, but well-drained soil

→ One of the early heralds of spring, winter hazel produces fragrant and buttery-yellow bell-shaped flowers on bare branches in late January and February. To some people these look like golden earrings.

There are two kinds worth getting to know: *Corylopsis pauciflora* (buttercup winter hazel), which is native to Taiwan and Japan, and *C. spicata* (spike winter hazel). Some gardeners consider *C. pauciflora* a more refined version of forsythia, which has brighter yellow flowers that last a lot longer.

After blooming, winter hazel covers itself with small, toothed leaves that have a touch of reddish purple to them. They turn yellow in fall.

C. pauciflora benefits when sheltered from icy blasts of wind or excessive rain in winter and blooms much better if protected from late frosts.

Once it is established, winter hazel sometimes will produce a second flush of flowers in September. It can be easily accommodated in the shrub border, ideally alongside deciduous trees such as the vine maple or saucer magnolia (page 51).

FEBRUARY

TYPE
bulb

SIZE
4 inches (10 cm)

LOCATION
full sun to part shade

CONDITIONS
average, well-drained soil

Crocus

→ This is such a familiar and uncomplicated flower that it is easy to overlook its value as one of the most beautiful and earliest blooming. The more I garden the more I realize the importance of flowering bulbs to provide consistent and continuous flowers in the garden. The humble crocus is certainly one we cannot afford to ignore.

There are 70 species in the genus, but the most popular kinds today are hybrids that bear very little resemblance to their ancestors, many of which are native to the Balkans, Hungary, Bulgaria and Greece.

There are large-flowering crocuses and the early-blooming "snow crocus." A selection from both categories will give you several weeks of colour. They always look best planted in clumps in large numbers. Most modern types come in shades of yellow, purple or white, although some cultivars have been bred to have stripes.

The snow crocus is the first to bloom in late winter. Top cultivars are 'Goldilocks', 'Ruby Giant' and 'Romance'. Species crocuses are also popular; 'Gypsy Girl' and 'Lady Killer' are two of the most striking, and 'Cream Beauty' is an exceptionally beautiful pale yellow.

They should be planted 3 to 4 inches (7.5 to 10 cm) deep in fall at the same time as other spring-flowering bulbs. Crocus bulbs can also be sprinkled across lawns and then planted where they fall to achieve a natural look in spring.

FEBRUARY

Edgeworthia chrysantha

PAPER BUSH

TYPE
shrub

SIZE
*4 to 6 feet
(1.2 to 1.8 m)*

LOCATION
full sun to light shade

CONDITIONS
*moist but well-
drained soil*

→ This deciduous shrub is a bit of a collector's item. You don't see it much in coastal gardens, partly because it is slightly tender unless planted in a protected spot, and partly because it is not widely known or seen when it is at its most attractive—in full bloom.

This shrub, which is native to the woodlands of China, is admired for its super-fragrant yellow daphne-like flowers that usually appear in late winter before the long, narrow tropical-looking leaves emerge. The cinnamon-coloured branches grow in a distinctive three-stem pattern. The bark is used in Japan to make high quality paper for bank notes.

Tolerant of mild frosts, edgeworthia is able to survive provided temperatures don't dip below 23°F (–5°C). If grown in a container and brought indoors for shelter over winter, the flowers will bloom earlier and can be enjoyed without the risk of being spoiled by rain or frosts. You will sometimes find it labelled *Edgeworthia papyrifera* ("paper-bearing"), but this is actually a different plant.

'Rubra' is a cultivar with bright red flowers that was introduced in Canada in 1996. 'Bhutan's Gold' is another selection that is more delicate with smaller, narrower leaves, but equally fragrant flowers, while 'Red Dragon' has orange-red flowers.

FEBRUARY

TYPE
perennial

SIZE
3 to 4 feet (90 cm to 1.2 m)

LOCATION
full sun

CONDITIONS
average, well-drained soil

Euphorbia characias wulfenii

SPURGE

→ This stately member of the spurge family not only stays green all year round, but it also produces gorgeous chartreuse multi-eyed flower heads from February to March. It has graceful spear-shaped blue-green foliage, and its flowers hang around for a long time and add colour and texture to the garden.

One of the best new introductions is 'Glacier Blue', which grows 18 inches (45 cm) high and has lovely blue-grey foliage with a creamy edge. 'Humpty Dumpty' is another first-class dwarf form that grows to 2 feet (60 cm). Two other excellent cultivars of *Euphorbia characias* are 'Portuguese Velvet', which has velvet-like leaves and grows to 2 feet (60 cm), and 'Tasmanian Tiger', which has green and white variegated leaves and grows to 3 feet (90 cm).

Other great euphorbias worth checking out:

- *E. myrsinites* (donkey tail spurge, page 106) has silver-blue leaves, chartreuse flowers and a cascading habit. It's useful for growing on sunny banks or over low walls.
- *E. amygdaloides* 'Purpurea' (wood spurge) has foliage that is heavily tinged with purple.
- *E.* 'Blackbird' has exceptionally deep purple (almost black) foliage.
- *E.* 'Shorty' has beautiful rosy tips in fall, followed by bright yellow flowers in spring.
- *E. amygdaloides* 'Robbiae' (Mrs. Robb's Bonnet) has sturdy, rosette-like green foliage.
- *E. dulcis* 'Chameleon' changes colour during the year from purplish green to burgundy-purple to dark green.
- *E.* × *martinii* 'Rudolph' has bright red bracts in winter, and yellow-green flowers with red centres in spring.
- *E. griffithii* 'Fireglow' has orange-red flowers and red-tinted leaves.
- *E. polychroma* (cushion spurge) produces an attractive mound of sulphur-yellow flowers.

FEBRUARY

TYPE
bulb

SIZE
4 to 6 inches
(10 to 15 cm)

LOCATION
full sun to part shade

CONDITIONS
fertile and moist but
well-drained soil

Galanthus

SNOWDROP

→ In the dreary days of January and February, is there a more uplifting sight than a clump of snowdrops defiantly blooming and proclaiming that spring is very near?

The snowdrop—with its small, nodding white flowers—makes such an elegant arrival that it has achieved a cultlike following in Britain where it has become popular to collect as many kinds as possible. And it may surprise you to know that there are a lot of cultivars—at least five hundred at last count.

There's 'Ketton', a tall robust snowdrop with grey-green leaves, 'Trym', a pixie-hatted variety with emerald markings, 'Hill Poe' with an inner rosette and 'Richard Ayres', which is taller than most and has larger flowers. *Galanthus reginae-olgae* actually flowers as early as October and will seed in drier sunny soils.

There are two main species sold at garden centres: *G. nivalis* and *G. elwesii*. There is also a popular "double flowered" cultivar called 'Flore Pleno' that has green highlights on the creamy white petals.

An ideal naturalizing bulb that flowers every year and expands to produce colonies, snowdrops are best planted "in the green," which means they are best planted after being started in small pots. But you can, of course, plant them with your other spring-flowering bulbs in September or October. Plant snowdrops 4 inches (10 cm) deep. Add manure and a handful of bone meal when you plant them.

They are best situated under deciduous trees and shrubs, at the base of hedges, over banks and berms, in among ground-cover ivy and in winter pots and planters.

Snowdrops hate to be disturbed, so once you've got a colony established it is best to leave it and allow it to expand in its own time.

FEBRUARY

Helleborus foetidus

STINKING HELLEBORE

→ This plant is not stinky at all—unless you put your nose very close to the vaguely skunky-smelling flowers. These yellowish green flowers develop in mid-winter, open in February and last through March and April.

But it is the beautiful architectural evergreen foliage that makes this woodland plant so admirable and useful for adding year-round interest. And it has the added bonus of flowers in late winter.

Top cultivars are 'Wester Flisk', which has red tinted leaves, 'Green Gnome', 'Miss Jekyll' and 'Piccadilly'. There is also a cultivar with golden foliage called 'Gold Bullion'.

Good companions include primula, dwarf daffodil, grape hyacinth and hardy cyclamen.

A must-have for the winter garden, *Helleborus foetidus* would make a nice start to a hellebore collection that should also include *H. argutifolius* (Corsican hellebore) and *H. × sternii* (both on page 14).

TYPE
perennial

SIZE
*18 to 24 inches
(45 to 60 cm)*

LOCATION
full sun to part shade

CONDITIONS
average, well-drained soil

FEBRUARY

Jasminum nudiflorum

WINTER JASMINE

TYPE
semi-clinging vine

SIZE
6 to 10 feet
(1.8 to 3 m)

LOCATION
full sun to part shade

CONDITIONS
well-drained soil

→ Brought to Europe from China in the mid-1800s, this deciduous, semi-clinging vine is valued for the bright yellow, trumpet-shaped flowers it produces on bare stems.

Hardy to Zone 6, it makes an attractive addition to the winter garden along with witch hazel, pink viburnum, skimmia, sarcococca, winter daphne and early-flowering hellebores.

The slender, willow-like stems require support if the plant is grown against a wall or fence as it does not twine naturally as do other jasmines and climbing vines. On the ground, it can be left to scramble up a bank or tumble freely over a low wall. It can be trained to a desired height and then allowed to cascade.

Grow winter jasmine close to the house or against a fence or trellis where the bright flowers can be most appreciated. Hard frosts can damage the flowers, so some protection is necessary if planted in an exposed area. Since the flowers are not fragrant, it is not necessary to plant winter jasmine for close access.

Juniperus squamata 'Blue Star'
BLUE STAR JUNIPER

→ The perfect dwarf conifer for growing in either a container or a drought-tolerant plant border, the 'Blue Star' juniper is a superior cultivar that has blue-green foliage with a silvery sparkle to it.

Developed in Holland in the 1950s, it was an offshoot of its already popular parent, *Juniperus squamata* 'Meyeri', yet it was not introduced to garden centres until at least a decade later.

Highly disease resistant, it is an excellent choice for a rock garden or a low-maintenance garden where space is limited. It is a natural companion for heathers, alpine plants and cool-season ornamental grasses that retain their colour all year.

For a beautiful, slender, column-shaped juniper, choose 'Skyrocket', which grows 8 to 10 feet (2.5 to 3 m) in ten years, and can eventually reach 25 feet (7.5 m).

Two other top names are 'Wichita Blue' and 'Blue Arrow', both of which are especially suited to the small garden. The common juniper (*J. communis*) also offers a few special, elegant, cigar-shaped cultivars, notably 'Compressa', 'Sentinel' and 'Hibernica'.

TYPE
shrub

SIZE
2 to 3 feet
(60 to 90 cm)

LOCATION
full sun

CONDITIONS
average, well-drained soil

FEBRUARY

Manglietia insignis

RED LOTUS TREE

TYPE
tree

SIZE
*25 to 40 feet
(7.5 to 12 m)*

LOCATION
full sun to part shade

CONDITIONS
average, well-drained soil

→ A rare sight in coastal gardens, *Manglietia insignis* has wonderful pale pink flowers with thick succulent-like petals from late spring through summer. The flowers are not produced all at once, but sporadically, opening slowly in different places all over the tree over a couple of months.

But this tree, which is related to the magnolia family and is sometimes called "an evergreen magnolia," also has very attractive evergreen foliage. This is why I have included it in this month—the flowers are great, but the supple, lanceolate leaves are green all year round, which means they provide colour and structure in the garden during winter, especially in the dreary days of February.

Native to western China, the Himalayas and Burma, the flower buds have a beauty of their own before they open; they are reddish green and stand perfectly erect on the branches, like candles.

I have grown this in my garden on the cooler, north side of the house for more than ten years. It started out as a small shrub, but I am glad I moved it early on to its present location. It now provides shade and privacy for our deck and also has plenty of space above to grow.

TYPE
shrub

SIZE
*2 to 3 feet
(60 to 90 cm)*

LOCATION
part shade

CONDITIONS
acidic, well-drained soil

Rhododendron moupinense

RHODODENDRON

→ With the right selection it is possible to have rhododendrons in bloom for seven months of the year. Kick off the sequence with the earliest bloomers, ones that burst into flower towards the end of winter.

Rhododendron moupinense is one of the first to bloom in coastal gardens, often producing its white flowers as early as January.

R. 'Christmas Cheer' and *R. lutescens* are also early bloomers. Despite its name, 'Christmas Cheer' doesn't flower at Christmas but produces cheerful pink blooms in February. *R. lutescens* has willow-like leaves and produces pale yellow flowers while *R.* 'Cilpinense' (blush pink) and *R. arboretum* (pink) are two more February bloomers.

R. barbatum and *R. thompsonii* (two great reds) bloom next in March, followed in April by 'PJM', one of the most popular of all rhodos. The foliage of 'PJM' turns a rich chocolate colour in winter, then turns green again in spring. The flowers are rosy purple.

April and May are prime months for rhododendrons and azaleas. Visit the garden centre and pick the colour and size you like best for your garden.

A lot of people don't realize that there are also rhodos that bloom in June and as late as July. 'Golden Ruby' offers a fascinating combination of strong red buds that open to waxy golden-yellow flowers in June, and *R. minus*, a native to the southeastern US, has either pink or white flowers. *R. maximum*, a large shrub that can grow to 15 feet (4.5 m), starts blooming in early July, producing pink flowers that last for at least three weeks.

FEBRUARY

MARCH

TO-DO LIST

○ *Aerate lawns to revitalize grass. Overseed bare spots. Eliminate moss by liming, improving drainage and creating more light through judicious pruning.*

○ *Or, sow seed or lay turf for your new lawn. The best grass seed for coastal gardens is a mixture of 60 percent perennial rye and a 40 percent blend of creeping red fescue and blue grass.*

- ○ If crows and skunks have damaged your lawn in their search for chafer beetles, consider an alternative: low-maintenance ground cover such as heather, ornamental grass, sedum, thyme and blue star creeper.
- ○ Divide large clumps of perennials by lifting and cutting them into two or more pieces. Replant immediately.
- ○ Clean up ornamental grasses, cutting summer-flowering varieties to the ground and giving cool-season varieties a haircut.
- ○ When you see forsythia in bloom, do the final pruning of hybrid tea and floribunda roses.
- ○ Put down organic mulch to improve soil structure and to reduce moisture loss through evaporation in summer.
- ○ Plant new perennials, shrubs, hedges, vines and trees, some of which will already be in bloom.
- ○ Plant bare-root roses. You'll already find a good selection at garden centres.
- ○ Buy and plant a rhododendron. Pick out your favourite from the many you'll see in bloom from now until the end of May.
- ○ Sow radishes, spinach, fennel, parsley, cauliflower, cabbage, potatoes, broccoli and carrots.
- ○ Eliminate weeds and hunt for slugs; these are two chores that will pay major dividends later.

MARCH

Adiantum pedatum var. *aleuticum*

MAIDENHAIR FERN

TYPE
perennial

SIZE
2 feet (60 cm)

LOCATION
part shade

CONDITIONS
moist but well-drained soil

→ Ferns are wonderful foliage plants. Along with hostas, they are the royalty of shade plants. Their main role in the garden is to provide architectural form, texture and contrast. We don't expect them to have colourful flowers, although some have lovely, patterned fronds. We mainly appreciate them for their reliable, long-lasting greenness and dependable structure.

Adiantum aleuticum, the graceful maidenhair fern, has delicate fan-shaped fronds with black ribs and stems. It is an indispensable plant for adding a light, airy, textural touch to shady areas around trees and shrubs.

Athyrium niponicum 'Pictum' (Japanese painted fern) is a more decorative fern also well worth finding a spot for. Named the Perennial of the Year in 2004 by the Perennial Plant Association, it has deep green fronds that have a decorative metallic silver-grey look with touches of red and blue. It grows to 18 inches (45 cm) high and will multiply to form a clump 2 feet (60 cm) wide.

MARCH

Anemone nemorosa

WOOD ANEMONE

→ Wood anemones are ideal for spreading under trees and shrubs to produce lovely white, blue or pale pink star-shaped flowers above low mounds of lush green leaves.

Native to Britain, where it has long become a woodland favourite, *Anemone nemerosa* develops from a small, slender rhizome that has the desire to colonize by quickly spreading just below the surface of leaf litter. It combines very well with spring-flowering bulbs such as grape hyacinth (page 53) and dwarf narcissus (page 54) as well as hellebores, primulas and hostas.

Top cultivars are 'Robinsoniana' (pale blue), 'Allenii' (lavender blue), 'Hilda' (white) and 'Green Fingers' (clusters of green petals inside white flowers).

A. blanda and *A. coronaria* are two other popular species that are sold as bulbs that are being planted in the fall. Native to the Mediterranean region, they produce beautiful blue, white and pink flowers that grow 6 inches (15 cm) high in spring.

'Blue Star', 'Rosea' and 'White Splendour' are outstanding varieties of *A. blanda*, while 'Blue Poppy', 'His Excellency' (red) and 'Sylphide' (pink) are favourite forms of *A. coronaria*. The latter are also known as "de Caen" hybrids after Caen in France where they were first developed.

TYPE
perennial

SIZE
6 to 8 inches
(15 to 20 cm)

LOCATION
full sun to part shade

CONDITIONS
moist but well-drained soil

MARCH

Betula pendula 'Youngii'

YOUNG'S BIRCH

TYPE
tree

SIZE
*6 to 8 feet
(1.8 to 2.5 m)*

LOCATION
full sun to part shade

CONDITIONS
*moist but well-
drained soil*

→ The ideal tree for the small courtyard or townhouse garden, Young's birch has an attractive umbrella shape that allows it to fit perfectly at the side of a pond or flower bed. It can also be grown very successfully in a container.

It is usually sold as a weeping standard, grafted onto the trunk about 6 to 8 feet (1.8 to 2.5 m) off the ground. It soon forms an attractive umbrella shape that can look particularly handsome next to a small pond or as the centrepiece in a flower bed.

Some say the roots of birch trees are notorious for getting into and blocking drains, but the roots of Young's birch are very shallow, which means it is perfectly safe to plant. The branches will inevitably drape to the ground, hiding the silvery-white trunk, but with a little judicious pruning the curtain of this canopy can easily be raised.

Other popular weeping trees to consider:

- *Salix caprea* 'Kilmarnock' (Kilmarnock willow), the weeping pussy willow tree, which grows 6 feet (1.8 m) high
- *Cedrus atlantica* 'Glauca Pendula' (Weeping Blue Atlas cedar), which has been used to add a dramatic look to an entrance, arbour or pergola and grows 15 to 30 feet (4.5 to 9 m)
- *C. deodara* (Deodar cedar), which looks like such a graceful, small tree as a baby but will quickly grow to a giant of 50 feet (15 m)

TYPE
shrub

SIZE
*3 to 4 feet
(90 cm to 1.2 m)*

LOCATION
full sun to part shade

CONDITIONS
average, well-drained soil

Buxus sempervirens

ENGLISH BOX, COMMON BOX, BOXWOOD

→ There's nothing quite like a low, well-clipped evergreen boxwood hedge to give your garden a classical elegance.

Boxwood is still mostly used as edging for rose or herb gardens or to define the edges of a flower border. But it is also used for topiary and can be clipped into various attractive shapes such as pyramids, cones and squares, as well as into assorted creatures. It also has been used very effectively in containers to create architectural accents such as large round "box balls."

Buxus sempervirens 'Suffruticosa' (true dwarf boxwood) is a slow-growing cultivar. It can take 20 years to grow to 4 feet (1.2 m). (Boxwood hedges at Powis Castle in Wales have reached 19 feet (5.8 m) after more than a hundred years of growth.) This is the best kind for edges, parterres, knot gardens and borders, and ideal for enclosing a small formal rose garden or herb garden.

Korean small-leafed boxwood (*B. microphylla* var. *koreana*) grows faster than common English box (*B. sempervirens*), but it doesn't like wet winters. It is best suited to drier areas where the soil is less acidic. Top varieties are 'Winter Gem' and 'Morris Midget'.

Other popular varieties of boxwood are 'Green Velvet', 'Green Beauty', 'Green Mound', 'Green Mountain' and 'Winter Green'.

MARCH

TYPE
shrub

SIZE
*6 to 12 feet
(1.8 to 3.5 m)*

LOCATION
part sun to light shade

CONDITIONS
*moist but well-
drained soil*

Camellia japonica

JAPANESE CAMELLIA

→ When the weather cooperates, and when its flowers are not damaged by frost or rain, *Camellia japonica* in full bloom is a sensational sight.

There are hundreds of cultivars of this popular broad-leaved evergreen, offering an impressive range of flower colours from candy pinks to bright reds, golden yellows to pure whites, and even red and white stripes.

The flowers are much admired, but so is the shrub's glossy green foliage that is useful for giving the garden year-round structure.

Native to Japan, China and parts of Malaysia and India, camellias are ideal plants for woodland gardens along with other acid-loving shrubs such as rhododendron, kalmia and azalea.

Camellia benefits from being mulched to protect the relatively shallow roots. The shrub is best planted where it will receive good air circulation, which can help prevent mildew problems.

Top cultivars are 'April Kiss', 'Adolphe Audusson', 'Alba Plena', 'Jury's Yellow', 'Chandleri', 'April Dawn', 'April Tryst', 'Nuccio's Pearl' and 'Winter's Snowman'.

While *C. japonica* is the most popular species with the most cultivars, there are other kinds worth checking out, including cultivars of *C. williamsii* such as 'Donation', an all-time favourite with soft-pink flowers, and 'Golden Spangles', which has distinctive variegated foliage. There is also the winter-flowering *C. sasanqua* (page 230), which offers blooms from November to January.

MARCH

Cercis canadensis 'Forest Pansy'

REDBUD

→ This is the perfect deciduous flowering tree for a small- or medium-sized garden because it does not grow very tall and it offers more than one season of interest.

A cultivar of the popular native eastern redbud, 'Forest Pansy' is mostly admired for its lovely purple, heart-shaped leaves. But it has other attractive qualities.

In early spring, before the leaves appear, it produces clusters of tiny, rose-purple, pealike flowers for a couple of weeks. These are followed by seed pods that resemble snow peas.

In fall, the leaves turn an attractive reddish purple with touches of orange, making it a handsome foliage specimen too.

'Forest Pansy' can be grown in a container but seems to be happiest with its roots settled in the ground. It also prefers a cool winter rather than a prolonged wet one, so it appreciates a northern or eastern exposure.

TYPE
tree

SIZE
*20 to 30 feet
(6 to 9 m)*

LOCATION
part sun to light shade

CONDITIONS
average, well-drained soil

MARCH

Chaenomeles japonica

FLOWERING QUINCE, JAPANESE QUINCE

TYPE
shrub

SIZE
*6 to 10 feet
(1.8 to 3 m)*

LOCATION
full sun

CONDITIONS
*average, well-drained,
acidic soil*

→ Many people call this red-flowered shrub
"quince." Others refer to it as *Japonica*, as if
"japonica" were a genus. Real quince is *Cydonia
oblonga*, a tree in the apple family that produces
golden fruit. The word *japonica* in any name simply
means "native to Japan."

Chaenomeles has been a taxonomist's nightmare
for years—the shrub was first thought to be in the
pear family, then in the quince family, until it had
finally been given its own genus.

Now called "Japanese quince," it is valued for its
bright clusters of waxy red flowers that are borne
on bare branches in early spring. By fall, the shrub
produces a small, hard, greenish yellow fruit that is
too bitter to eat but can still be used to make jam
or jelly.

In Japan it is used for bonsai, despite its
prickly thorns. Here in coastal gardens it is often
espaliered against walls or fences, or simply grown
as a shrub or small tree.

Dicksonia antarctica

TASMANIAN TREE FERN

→ This plant goes well with a tropical garden theme because of its fabulous large fronds, which give it an exotic jungle-like look. It can be grown in a container or planted in a semi-shady spot in the garden.

It is designated as Zone 8, which means it needs protection from heavy frost and cold winds in most of the Pacific Northwest. The tree fern is native to Australia where it grows from southeastern Queensland to New South Wales and Tasmania. It is happiest in dappled shade with a carpet of mulch to retain moisture around its base.

All new growth starts from the crown of the plant. This can contain as many as 60 fronds. These unfurl in spring to form the large fronds. To protect it from frost in the winter, it is more important to wrap the crown rather than the thick trunklike stem, which grows at the rate of an inch (2.5 cm) a year.

TYPE
tree

SIZE
15 feet (4.5 m)

LOCATION
light shade

CONDITIONS
average, well-drained soil

MARCH

Forsythia × intermedia

FORSYTHIA

TYPE
shrub

SIZE
*10 to 15 feet
(3 to 4.5 m)*

LOCATION
full sun to part shade

CONDITIONS
average, well-drained soil

→ When you see the bright yellow flowers of forsythia in full bloom, you know that it's time to get out the secateurs and prune your roses.

While it is one of the best seasonal gardening guides, forsythia does have more value than acting as a mere alarm clock for rose growers. Not only does it provide a striking burst of spring colour with its stunning yellow flowers, it can be clipped to form a neat green barrier or background hedge in a mixed shrub border. It needs to be pruned every year for size and shape, immediately after flowering.

It gets its name from 18th-century Scottish horticulturist William Forsyth, a founding member of the Royal Horticultural Society. Forsythia is native to China and is a fuss-free, disease-resistant shrub.

Top cultivars are 'Fiesta', 'Spectabilis', 'Spring Glory', 'Golden Peep', 'Gold Tide' and 'Lynwood Gold'. 'Sunrise' is ideal for smaller gardens since it is more compact.

Don't plant it close to pink-flowered cherry trees if you want to avoid a hideous colour clash.

Helleborus orientalis

LENTEN ROSE

→ Coveted by plant connoisseurs, the Lenten rose ranks among the world's most desirable perennials. Cousin to the Christmas rose (*Helleborus niger*, page 246), it is more popular because its blooms, which appear during the weeks leading up to and during Easter, are more colourful and more visible. Flower colours range from burgundy and red to soft pink and pale yellow.

The old rule was that *H. orientalis* should be planted in dappled shade, but the current consensus of opinion is that it should be planted in part sun, especially in coastal gardens where there is often frequent cloud cover.

Most popular cultivars are hybrids marketed under the name *H. × hybridus*, which was named Perennial of the Year for 2005 by the Perennial Plant Association in the US.

Top cultivars are 'Ivory Prince', 'Red Lady', 'Royal Heritage' and 'Yellow Lady'. More unusual types are also available including 'Kingston Cardinal' (raspberry red) and 'Snow Bunting' (pure white).

Leaves sometimes obscure the flowers, but the foliage can be cut away to make the blooms more visible. The leaves will be replaced by new growth. To protect the flowers, some gardeners use cloches.

TYPE
perennial

SIZE
*12 to 18 inches
(30 to 45 cm)*

LOCATION
part shade to full sun

CONDITIONS
average, well-drained soil

MARCH

Iris reticulata

DWARF IRIS

→ Dwarf irises should be planted en masse along with snowdrops, crocuses and miniature daffodils and also squeezed into winter containers and liberally sprinkled throughout rockeries.

The two most popular cultivars are 'Harmony', with its royal blue and purple petals and a bright yellow blotch, and 'J. S. Dijt', which has deep purple petals, black leopard spots and a yellow stripe.

Other top varieties are 'Joyce', 'Springtime', 'Gordon' and 'Cantab', which has sky-blue petals. *Iris danfordiae* is a member of the same family with canary-yellow flowers.

Plant *I. reticulata* 4 inches (10 cm) deep in the fall. They prefer neutral soil but thrive without fuss in acidic soils of coastal gardens. Surround plants with sharp grit to discourage snails and slugs. They can also be tucked among blue grasses or throughout a carpet of thyme.

TYPE *bulb*

SIZE *4 to 6 inches (10 to 15 cm)*

LOCATION *full sun to part shade*

CONDITIONS *average, well-drained soil*

Isotoma fluviatilis

BLUE STAR CREEPER

→ A superb, mat-forming plant, blue star creeper can be used to fill gaps between paving stones or as part of a tapestry when replacing a lawn with a low-maintenance flower bed.

Living up to its name, it produces masses of tiny, star-shaped blue flowers that creep over and soften the edges of pavers. This plant is often incorrectly labelled *Laurentia fluviatilis*. 'Kelsey Blue' is a popular cultivar.

Other great gap and crevice fillers are *Aubrieta* ('Red Carpet', 'Blue Carpet' and 'Dr. Mules'), *Saponaria* (alpine soapwort) and *Sedum spathulifolium* 'Cape Blanco' or *Sedum oreganum*. *Lithodora diffusa* 'Grace Ward' is an old favourite. It is a reliable, tough-as-nails ground cover with bright, sky-blue flowers and attractive evergreen foliage. It grows 4 to 6 inches (10 to 15 cm) high.

TYPE *perennial*

SIZE *2 to 3 inches (5 to 7.5 cm)*

LOCATION *full sun to part shade*

CONDITIONS *average, well-drained soil*

MARCH

TYPE
tree

SIZE
*10 to 25 feet
(3 to 7.5 m)*

LOCATION
full sun to part shade

CONDITIONS
fertile, well-drained soil

Magnolia soulangeana

SAUCER MAGNOLIA

→ So many trees and shrubs bloom in March—cherry trees, forsythia, camellias, pieris—but saucer magnolias (cultivars of *Magnolia soulangeana*) always hold their own with their extraordinary purple and white goblet-shaped blooms.

English garden guru, the late Christopher Lloyd, called magnolias "the most glamorous and effective of all shrubs or trees." He added, "There is room for at least one specimen in every garden."

These trees produce flowers on bare branches from March to April. Top cultivars are 'Coates', 'Alexandrina', 'Rustica Rubra' and 'Lennei'. 'Coates', which has deep lavender flowers, is considered the best of the bunch.

A relatively slow-growing tree or shrub, its natural habit is to grow almost as wide as it is tall, so it is important to give it a decent amount of room to expand. It is a natural partner for rhododendron and azalea, as well as for spring-flowering shrubs such as *Pieris japonica* (page 57) and *Ribes sanguineum* (page 87).

Prune after flowering, or not at all. Late-summer pruning will reduce the number of flowers in spring.

For smaller gardens, there is the Little Girl series of hybrids, all of which grow 8 to 10 feet (2.5 to 3 m) high: 'Jane', 'Judy', 'Pinkie', 'Randy', 'Ricki', 'Ann', 'Betty' and 'Susan'.

Other highly rated magnolias for coastal gardens to consider include 'Vulcan' (ruby red), 'Galaxy' (reddish purple) and 'Caerhays Belle' (salmon pink).

MARCH

Magnolia stellata

STAR MAGNOLIA

TYPE
tree

SIZE
10 to 15 feet
(3 to 4.5 m)

LOCATION
full sun to part shade

CONDITIONS
*moist but well-
drained soil*

→ When the bright yellow flowers of forsythia begin to lose their freshness, the star magnolia arrives on the scene to lift the landscape again to new heights of interest and beauty.

The brilliantly white star-shaped flowers of this magnolia are especially breathtaking when surrounded by a carpet of blue vinca, chiondoxa or muscari. The flowers are also more noticeable if the tree is grown against a dark backdrop of yew or cedar hedging.

Magnolia stellata is native to Japan, and is one of the prettiest trees in the magnolia family and one of the easiest to accommodate in the average-size garden. It can be grown either as a regular-shaped tree or in a less formal bush form.

The top cultivar is 'Royal Star', but also look for 'Waterlily', which blooms a little later, and 'Rosea', which has blush-pink flowers. In cooler gardens, 'Centennial' is a better choice, having been bred specifically for hardiness.

Magnolia fans tend to rate *M. kobus* more highly because of its larger canopy of white flowers, but others say the star magnolia has cleaner, purer white flowers. In reality, both magnolias are terrific.

Muscari armeniacum

GRAPE HYACINTH

→ After winter we crave colour in the garden. Snowdrops and crocuses are a welcome sight, but few early spring-flowering bulbs are as long-lasting or as useful throughout the garden as the simple grape hyacinth. Its lack of complexity and pretension along with its total reliability make it all the more likable.

Muscari gets its common name from its tiny blue flowers that are arranged in grapelike clusters. Native to southern Europe and western Asia where it flourishes on grassy hillsides, muscari naturalizes effortlessly when scattered throughout the garden under trees and shrubs or intermingled in the perennial border.

You'll find two kinds at the garden centre: *Muscari armeniacum* and *M. latifolium*. Both are terrific, but the latter has eye-catching, two-tone blue spikes for something a little different. *M. plumosum* is a novel species with feathery purple plumes.

Also check out the old-fashioned English bluebell (*Scilla non-scripta* or *Hyacinthoides non-scripta*) and the Spanish bluebell (*S. campanulata* or *H. hispanica* or *Endymion hispanicus*). The latter has stiffer, more upright stems than the English bluebell and equally beautiful flowers, although with little or no fragrance. However, the Spanish bluebell is easier to find at most garden centres.

TYPE
bulb

SIZE
6 inches (15 cm)

LOCATION
full sun to part shade

CONDITIONS
average, well-drained soil

MARCH

Narcissus

MINIATURE DAFFODIL

TYPE
bulb

SIZE
*8 to 10 inches
(20 to 25 cm)*

LOCATION
full sun to part shade

CONDITIONS
average, well-drained soil

→ The beauty of dwarf narcissus is that they flower beautifully, don't flop over and when they're finished blooming they don't leave an unsightly mess.

Rock garden narcissus are the first to bloom in February and last through to March. 'Bell Song' has white petals and a pale-pink cup, 'February Gold' is a warm yellow, 'Pipit' is more lemon yellow while 'Suzy' has yellow petals and a bright orange cup. Others to consider include 'Quail', 'Rip Van Winkle', 'Segovia', 'Thalia' and 'Topolino'. Most have a light fragrance.

Most popular are the April-blooming miniatures: 'Jack Snipe', 'Jetfire' and 'Tete a Tete'.

Complete your collection with some of the mid-spring dwarf narcissus. Names to look for include 'Baby Moon', 'Hawera', 'Minnow', 'Pacific Coast', 'Sundial' and 'Little Gem'. My favourites are the ones with fragrance: 'Baby Moon' and 'Hawera'.

Miniature daffs are ideally planted in dense clumps under trees and shrubs in parts of the perennial border that are slow to get going in spring.

Plant miniature narcissus in late September through to mid-October when the soil is still relatively warm and able to promote good root development. They make excellent partners for snowdrops, dwarf irises and hyacinths.

Ophiopogon planiscapus 'Nigrescens'

BLACK MONDO GRASS, BLACK LILYTURF

→ Black is a fun colour to play with in the garden. It adds a sense of drama, novelty and curiosity. You'd be surprised how striking some flower combinations can be when you dare to mix in a little black.

Ophiopogon planiscapus 'Nigrescens' produces spidery clumps of thin, jet-black, straplike leaves and tiny, pink-mauve flowers, which are followed by small black berries.

Many gardeners use it as either a ground cover or in containers to achieve dynamic colour contrast.

An excellent planting idea is to use black mondo grass around the white trunk of a Himalayan birch, or in a container with the yellow leaves of creeping jenny (*Lysimachia nummularia*, page 199) or the silver foliage of *Lamium maculatum*.

TYPE
ornamental grass

SIZE
*6 to 8 inches
(15 to 20 cm)*

LOCATION
full sun to part shade

CONDITIONS
moist but well-drained soil

MARCH

Pachysandra terminalis

JAPANESE SPURGE

TYPE
perennial

SIZE
6 to 10 inches
(15 to 25 cm)

LOCATION
part shade to full shade

CONDITIONS
average, well-drained soil

→ A popular rule of gardening is that all soil should be covered, especially in summer when the sun can suck the life-giving moisture from the ground and put your plants under stress. Most of us use grass for this purpose while mulch is more routinely spread to protect soil around perennials in borders.

If you have large areas of exposed soil under trees or shrubs, plant a reliable ground cover, preferably one that not only holds and protects the soil, suppresses weeds and reduces moisture loss, but also has attractive flowers or foliage.

Pachysandra terminalis (Japanese spurge) does a great job. Hardy and drought tolerant, it also has fragrant, creamy white flowers in late spring. Top cultivars are 'Green Carpet', 'Green Sheen' and 'Variegata', which has green leaves with creamy white edges.

Also consider: *Vinca minor* (periwinkle), probably the most widely grown ground cover with its dainty lilac-blue flowers and small, glossy evergreen leaves; *Ajuga reptans* (bugleweed), a creeping plant with small, thin, rounded leaves; *Bergenia cordifolia* (giant rockfoil, or large-leaved saxifrage) with large, leathery, bright green leaves that turn coppery red in fall; and *Epimedium* (bishop's hat, or barrenwort) with heart-shaped leaves.

Photinia × *fraseri*
RED-TIPPED PHOTINIA

→ Photinia is an excellent shrub that is often unfairly dismissed as too common because it has been so widely planted. Nevertheless, it makes a superb hedge and can even be grown into an attractive tree-form or as a container specimen. Or it can be routinely sheared into a short hedge 3 to 4 feet (90 cm to 1.2 m) high.

The new foliage in spring is bright red and is especially handsome amid already established glossy leaves, which stay green all year round in coastal gardens.

Disease resistant and tolerant of most soil conditions, photinia is a totally fuss-free shrub that can even be used for topiary if desired.

The top cultivar is 'Red Robin', which won the Royal Horticultural Society's Award of Garden Merit, but you could ask for 'Robusta' or 'Birmingham'.

TYPE *shrub*

SIZE *10 to 15 feet (3 to 4.5 m)*

LOCATION *full sun to part shade*

CONDITIONS *average, well-drained soil*

Pieris japonica
LILY-OF-THE-VALLEY SHRUB

→ Pieris, a first-class evergreen shrub that originates from the Himalayas, has two key characteristics. The first is the beauty of its new foliage, which is bright red or salmon pink in early spring, and slowly turns green by summer. The second is its abundant clusters of tiny, white, bell-shaped, lily-of-the-valley-like flowers, from which pieris gets its common name.

'Japonica' is the most commonly planted; 'Forest Flame' is popular because of its new foliage, which is a brilliant scarlet-red. But there are several other fine cultivars such as 'Mountain Fire', 'Valley Rose', 'Flaming Silver' and 'Variegata' (which has green and white leaves). If space is limited, there are dwarf forms such as 'Cavatine', 'Bisbee Dwarf' or 'Prelude'.

TYPE *shrub*

SIZE *6 to 8 feet (1.8 to 2.5 m)*

LOCATION *full sun to light shade*

CONDITIONS *average, well-drained soil*

MARCH

Primula denticulata

DRUMSTICK PRIMULA

TYPE
perennial

SIZE
12 inches (30 cm)

LOCATION
light shade

CONDITIONS
moist but well-drained soil

→ With large, spherical clusters of flowers at the top of skinny green stems (which give them the appearance of drumsticks), *Primula denticulata* brings the exotic charm of a Himalayan mountainside to your backyard.

They are among the first primroses to bloom in spring, and flowers come in shades of white, blue, lilac and pink. Varieties to look for include 'Alba' (white), 'Rubin' (rose-pink) and 'Blue Selection' (lilac to deep blue). You will easily spot them because of their distinctive shape.

Rain can spoil the blooms, which is why some gardeners grow them under cover in an alpine house or other protected area.

Also find room for *Primula sieboldii* (Japanese star primrose), another collector's item that grows to 9 inches (23 cm) tall and produces fabulous white, pink, magenta or purple flowers. Top names are 'Geisha Girl' (shocking pink), 'Mikado' (purple) and 'Snowflake' (pure white). Grow them in a container or rock garden.

MARCH

TYPE
perennial

SIZE
*4 to 6 inches
(10 to 15 cm)*

LOCATION
shade to part sun

CONDITIONS
moist but well-drained soil

Primula vulgaris

DOUBLE ENGLISH PRIMROSE

→ Poets have called the primrose many things over the centuries—"merry springtime's harbinger," "fairest flower," "firstling of the infant year"—and it is thought that the name itself comes from the medieval notion that it is the "prime rose," or the first flower of spring. These make first-rate plants for growing under deciduous trees and shrubs in woodland settings, and they bloom from March to May.

There are many kinds worth having in the garden, but the old-fashioned double English primroses are always reliable, disease resistant and easy to grow. They have multi-petalled, roselike flowers in a variety of colours like ruby red, violet-blue, light pink and bright buttercup yellow.

You'll mostly find hybrids of *Primula vulgaris*. 'Quaker's Bonnet' is one of the first to flower in spring with superbly subtle lavender-purple flowers. It probably dates back to the 18th century. More striking is 'Miss Indigo' with its deep purple flowers with silvery-white edges. There are many others worth checking out including 'April Rose' (deep red), 'Dawn Ansell' (white), 'Lilian Harvey' (rose-pink), 'Sunshine Susie' (golden yellow) and 'Sue Jervis' (muted peach).

Primulas are moisture lovers, thriving in cool, shady sites. The ideal location to grow primulas is on the east side of the house, perhaps under rhododendrons and deciduous trees and shrubs where they can soak up sunshine in spring. In the summer, morning sun won't hurt, but the midday or afternoon sun will scorch them.

Prunus × yedoensis 'Akebono'

YOSHINO CHERRY

→ One of the best ornamental flowering cherry trees, the Yoshino cherry pumps out masses of pink blooms, which only partly explains why it is the most commonly planted ornamental cherry in the Pacific Northwest. The Yoshino cherry is also well loved for its high resistance to disease.

In ten years it can grow 15 to 20 feet (4.5 to 6 m) high and the canopy can reach as wide as 25 to 30 feet (7.5 to 9 m).

Prunus × yedoensis has a lot of different cultivars, including the highly rated 'Shidare Yoshino' with its white flowers, but the blossoms of 'Akebono' are considered superior to all others.

TYPE *tree*

SIZE *15 to 20 feet (4.5 to 6 m)*

LOCATION *full sun to light shade*

CONDITIONS *average, well-drained soil*

Sedum rupestre 'Angelina'

SEDUM

→ Lawnless gardens are becoming increasingly popular along with the rise of xeriscape planting schemes, which are drought tolerant and aim for minimal use of water, making use of clever water-saving techniques such as mulching.

Sedum rupestre 'Angelina' is one of the plants widely used in such schemes because not only is it capable of surviving in poor soil without a lot of water, but it also has very attractive golden-yellow foliage.

It has a natural spreading habit, which makes it an effective carpeting ground cover. It will also cascade, so it can be used in hanging baskets, window boxes or troughs.

Other excellent sedums for using in lawn-replacement schemes in full sun include *S. spathulifolium* 'Cape Blanco', which has bluish grey foliage and yellow flowers, and *S. kamtschaticum* 'Variegatum'.

TYPE *perennial*

SIZE *4 to 6 inches (10 to 15 cm)*

LOCATION *full sun*

CONDITIONS *average, well-drained soil*

Sempervivum tectorum

HENS AND CHICKS, HOUSELEEKS

→ Often planted in bowls, troughs and strawberry pots, hens and chicks will flourish without care and attention for many years. It has attractive clusters of fleshy leaves, forming tightly compact rosettes.

Sempervivum tectorum also goes by the curious name St. Patrick's cabbage, but it gets its more common name hens and chicks from the fact that the mother plant develops small, baby rosettes at the side as it matures.

New hybrids have expanded the range of colours from the plain but attractive grey-green, to purple, olive green, pink and maroon. Although each rosette is only a few inches wide, they can spread to form a beautiful thick tapestry of colour, especially on the roof of a shed or in a well-drained trough. Top cultivars include 'Red Beauty', 'More Honey' and 'Oddity'.

Unlike echeverias and aeoniums, sempervivums can stay outdoors all winter, but they need to be protected from continual rainfall and waterlogged soil. Being monocarpic, the plant always dies after flowering, but it usually produces lots of "chicks" around the base so you won't lose the plant.

TYPE
perennial

SIZE
4 inches (10 cm)

LOCATION
full sun to part shade

CONDITIONS
average, well-drained soil

MARCH

Spiraea × bumalda 'Goldflame'
SPIREA

TYPE
shrub

SIZE
3 to 4 feet
(90 cm to 1.2 m)

LOCATION
full sun to light shade

CONDITIONS
average, well-drained soil

→ There are two main types of spirea—ones with white flowers in spring, and ones that have red-pink flowers in early summer. You could make room in your garden for one or the other, or both.

Spiraea × bumalda 'Goldflame' is an excellent choice. It is quick to leaf out in the spring, producing bronze leaves that turn golden yellow. These are followed by rose-red flower clusters that peak in June. The foliage is great for contrasting with other plants such as heuchera and euphorbia.

Other top cultivars include 'Magic Carpet' (foliage with gold, lime-green and red hues and plenty of pinkish purple flowers in midsummer), 'Anthony Waterer' (rose-pink flowers from July to September), 'Little Princess' (mint-green foliage and rose-pink flowers) and 'Goldmound'. All are ruggedly disease and pest resistant.

White-flowering kinds include *S. nipponica* 'Snowmound', which has an upright habit and arching branches and grows 4 to 8 feet (1.2 to 2.5 m), *S. thunbergii,* which has pure white flower clusters in April and grows to 5 feet (1.5 m) and *S. × vanhouttei* (bridal wreath spirea), which is a compact, upright, deciduous shrub that grows into a fountain shape about 6 feet (1.8 m) high and produces a dazzling cascade of snow-white flowers in May.

Stachys byzantina
LAMB'S EARS

Thuja occidentalis 'Smaragd'
HEDGING CEDAR

→ Of all the great foliage plants, lamb's ears continues to be the most widely used as a ground cover or decorative accent plant. It gets its common name from the soft, woolly texture of its leaves.

Top cultivars are 'Silver Carpet', 'Helen Von Stein' and 'Primrose Heron', which has chartreuse-yellow foliage rather than silvery grey. 'Silver Carpet' rarely blooms, so gardeners are spared the job of cutting down lanky flower stalks. 'Helen Von Stein' has bigger leaves.

If you like grey foliage you will also want to check out *Ballota pseudodictamnus*, which grows to 2 feet (60 cm) high and has oval-shaped grey-green leaves. Also check out the star members of the *Artemisia* family:

- *A. ludoviciana* 'Valerie Finnis' has soft, willowy silver-white leaves.
- *A. schmidtiana* 'Silver Mound' forms a small mound of soft feathery leaves.
- *A. stelleriana* 'Silver Brocade' is used as a carpeting ground cover.
- *A.* 'Powis Castle' has bushy, silver foliage and a non-invasive habit.

TYPE *perennial*

SIZE *6 to 10 inches (15 to 25 cm)*

LOCATION *full sun*

CONDITIONS *average, well-drained soil*

→ Many homeowners decide to plant a hedge in spring. On the West Coast, 'Smaragd' is the most popular choice. It grows quickly, has a high disease resistance and is more affordable than the more elegant but slower-growing yew (*Taxus* × *media*).

'Smaragd', which was developed in Denmark, is also very drought tolerant. It can be routinely topped and pruned every year to create a thick, lush, architectural hedge. Other top cultivars are 'Brandon', 'Degroots Spire', 'Holmstrup', 'Sherwood Forest' and 'Nigra'.

Other good hedging choices: *Photinia* × *fraseri*, which has cheerful red new growth, and can be kept as low as 3 feet (90 cm) to well over 10 feet (3 m); *Prunus laurocerasus* (Cherry laurel), with glossy, 5-inch-long (13 cm) leaves, and capable of reaching 15 feet (4.5 m) in ten years; and *Ilex* × *meserveae* (Meserve hybrid holly), which can provide a prickly barrier to thwart burglars and red berries for winter interest.

TYPE *shrub*

SIZE *10 to 15 feet (3 to 4.5 m)*

LOCATION *full sun to part shade*

CONDITIONS *average, well-drained soil*

APRIL

→ NOTES

TO-DO LIST

○ *Prune early-blooming shrubs, such as* Ribes sanguineum *and forsythia, after flowering.*

○ *Clip and tidy up winter-flowering heathers as they finish blooming.*

○ *Deadhead grape hyacinths, tulips and daffodils. Feed bulbs after flowering with 6-8-6 fertilizer.*

○ *Cut away old leaves around the Lenten rose* (Helleborus orientalis) *to expose the flowers.*

○ *Continue dividing and planting perennials as well as finding places for new trees and shrubs.*

○ *Plant seed potatoes, using certified virus-free stock, either whole or cut into pieces with two or three eyes— tiny indentations from which the sprouts will grow— facing up.*

○ *Plant beets, broccoli, carrots, celery, cauliflower, cabbage, kohlrabi, onions, parsnips, turnips, Swiss chard and lettuce.*

○ *Start tomato, zucchini and cucumber seeds indoors for transplanting outdoors in June. Pick early-ripening tomatoes—ones that ripen in 60 days or less—such as 'Tumbler', 'Sungold' and 'Sweet Million'. Other reliable picks include 'Siletz', 'Kootenai' and 'Oregon Spring'.*

○ *Get dahlia tubers started in recycled black plastic pots or milk cartons for transplanting in May.*

○ *Get control of the herbaceous border early, staking plants known for their floppy or unruly nature.*

○ *Plant hanging baskets, but keep them in a protected environment until May.*

TYPE
perennial

SIZE
3 feet (90 cm)

LOCATION
light shade

CONDITIONS
average, well-drained soil

Aquilegia vulgaris
COLUMBINE

➜ Sooner or later, all gardeners fall in love with columbine because of its seductively beautiful and intricate flowers, which come in a wide range of colours. The fact that columbine likes the cool, dappled shade of a woodland garden also gives it romantic appeal.

Aquilegia produce unique funnel-shaped flowers that are said to resemble a circle of doves when turned upside down. The plant's name is derived from the Latin word for *dove*, so perhaps there is something to it.

There are a variety of flower types including alpine, granny-bonnet, dwarf, Japanese and clematis. And there are various popular series such as McKana Giant Hybrids, Songbird, Barlow, Winky and Woodside.

The Woodside group is popular because of its golden or lime-green variegated foliage. Flowers can range from deep reddish pink to pale blue and mauve. 'Woodside Gold', one of the top cultivars, grows 1.5 to 2 feet (45 to 60 cm) high and has light pink flowers from April to May.

Other sought-after cultivars include members of the Barlow group ('Black Barlow', 'Blue Barlow', 'Nora Barlow' and 'Christa Barlow') and the clematis-flowered types like 'Clementine Rose' and 'Clementine Blue'.

Left to freely seed, they will naturalize in the garden and become perfect companions for shrubs such as spirea and azalea as well as early-blooming roses. Aquilegia also look excellent grown in the perennial border among stalwart performers such as *Alchemilla mollis*, campanula, dicentra, hosta, astrantia, hardy geranium and pulmonaria.

APRIL

Aubrieta deltoidea

FALSE ROCKCRESS

→ There's no shortage of wonderful rock garden plants that will fill crevices or provide a cascade of flowers over low retaining walls. Alpine soapwort (*Saponaria alpina*), rock candytuft (*Iberis sempervirens*), mountain alyssum (*Alyssum montanum*) and creeping donkey tail spurge (*Euphorbia myrsinites,* page 106) are a few favourites.

But rockcress (*Aubrieta*) is easily the most popular. It delivers masses of tiny pink, purple, blue, lavender or red flowers in April above a soft cushion of evergreen leaves.

It needs to be watered weekly when it is first planted but should never be allowed to sit in soggy soil. And once it has finished blooming, take your shears and trim it back. This will tidy it up and encourage sporadic re-blooming during summer. You can try to divide clumps to create new colonies, but it is far easier to sow seed or buy inexpensive small pots of new plants.

Top cultivars are 'Doctor Mules', 'Royal Red' and 'Cascade Blue', but there are dozens of others, including 'Argenteovariegata', a variety with variegated cream and white leaves.

TYPE
perennial

SIZE
4 inches (10 cm)

LOCATION
full sun

CONDITIONS
average, well-drained soil

APRIL

Berberis

BARBERRY

TYPE
shrub

SIZE
full sun to light shade

LOCATION
4 to 5 feet (1.2 to 1.5 m)

CONDITIONS
average, well-drained soil

→ This is the dreaded "prickle bush" of English schoolyards of yesteryear. It can be grown as a solid deciduous hedge, and tucked below a window it can be a deterrent to burglars. Regular pruning can keep it neat and tidy.

Popular cultivars are mostly varieties of *Berberis thunbergii* (Japanese barberry). Look for 'Rose Glow', which has purple-red leaves marbled with cream and pink highlights, and pale yellow flowers in spring that are followed by red berries in fall and winter. Also look for 'Atropurpurea', with dark, purplish brown foliage, and 'Aurea' (golden barberry), which has yellow foliage that turns shades of orange, red and gold in fall. 'Atropurpurea Nana' is a dwarf variety that only grows to 2 feet (60 cm).

The best evergreen barberry is 'Goldilocks', which produces golden-orange flowers in spring, and then occasionally from midsummer to fall. A slow-growing, medium- to large-sized shrub, it will reach 6 to 10 feet (1.8 to 3 m) if left unpruned.

Brunnera macrophylla 'Jack Frost'
SIBERIAN BUGLOSS, FALSE FORGET-ME-NOT

Camassia cusickii
CAMAS LILY

→ Nobody cared about Siberian bugloss until 'Jack Frost' came along. One of the best new cultivars to be introduced in the past ten years, it has fabulous foliage (beautiful heart-shaped silver leaves with delicate green veins) and even prettier flowers (dainty blue forget-me-not-like blooms) that continue for weeks and weeks.

As an added bonus, the leaves plump up when the flowers begin to fade, making them even more expressive.

A woodland plant, grow 'Jack Frost' where it will receive morning sun and afternoon shade since the leaves can scorch easily.

'Looking Glass' is a similar cultivar with leaves that are even more silvery. Both cultivars are excellent additions to the garden.

TYPE *perennial*

SIZE *12 to 14 inches (30 to 35 cm)*

LOCATION *light shade*

CONDITIONS *moist but well-drained soil*

→ Few sights are as beautiful as a spring meadow lavishly planted with blue camassia. This is an exceptional flower produced by a bulb.

In the home garden, it can be placed in the perennial border, where once it has finished blooming it can be replaced by other perennials such as astilbe or astrantia.

There are three key species: *Camassia cusickii*, *C. leichtlinii* and *C. quamash*. All are native to marshy meadowlands in the Pacific Northwest and produce similar star-shaped blue flowers.

C. cusickii is the most popular while *C. quamash* 'Blue Melody' is a darker blue cultivar with striking variegated foliage.

TYPE *bulb*

SIZE *3 feet (90 cm)*

LOCATION *full sun to part shade*

CONDITIONS *moist soil*

APRIL

TYPE
tree

SIZE
40 feet (12 m)

LOCATION
full sun to part shade

CONDITIONS
moist but well-drained soil

Cercidiphyllum japonicum

KATSURA

→ There are many beautiful spring-flowering trees—magnificent magnolias like *Magnolia sprengeri* 'Diva' and splendid ornamental cherries like *Prunus* 'Akebono'. But the katsura has a special appeal in spring because of the exceptional copper colour of its new leaves.

A handsome heart-shape, the leaves slowly turn a pleasant shade of green for summer, then change colour again in the fall, becoming bright apricot yellow with touches of red and pink.

With the warm air of late August, the leaves also give off a subtle toffee or burnt sugar aroma that lasts well into September.

Add to all of this the katsura's lovely overall shape and high disease resistance, as well as its reasonable drought tolerance—is it any surprise that it is such a popular street tree? It could also be argued that it offers four seasons of interest since it even looks wonderful with bare branches in winter, especially when draped with white lights for Christmas.

There are also two weeping forms of katsura: 'Pendula' and 'Morioka Weeping'. Both are capable of growing into wonderful shimmering waterfalls of leaves. They will grow 15 to 25 feet (4.5 to 7.5 m) in ten years. In fall, the foliage turns shades of orange. 'Morioka Weeping' has larger leaves and is considered more vigorous.

Corydalis lutea

YELLOW CORYDALIS

→ Looking for a non-stop blooming perennial? From the moment the first flowers appear in mid-spring, *Corydalis lutea* just keeps on producing clusters of tiny, yellow, tubular flowers above lush mounds of frothy foliage until the end of summer.

It has a habit of self-seeding everywhere, but this may be exactly what you want it to do. If not, you can either resign yourself to pulling out the seedlings, which you can give away to friends, or grow the plant only where its free-seeding habit is not going to be a problem. The benefits of growing corydalis outweigh the disadvantages.

Gardening connoisseurs covet the blue-flowering hybrids: 'Blue Panda', 'Pere David', 'China Blue' and 'Purple Leaf'. 'Blue Panda' was the first on the block, but 'Purple Leaf' has proved to be the most reliable. None of the blues, however, flower quite as profusely or as reliably as the yellow form.

TYPE
perennial

SIZE
*12 to 18 inches
(30 to 45 cm)*

LOCATION
part sun to light shade

CONDITIONS
average, well-drained soil

APRIL

Darmera peltata

UMBRELLA PLANT

TYPE
perennial

SIZE
*3 to 5 feet
(90 cm to 1.5 m)*

LOCATION
light shade

CONDITIONS
*moist but well-
drained soil*

→ You don't want every plant in your garden to look the same and have the same-sized leaves for precisely the same reason you want to vary the heights of plants in your garden: it makes things more visually interesting. It is good to have a few plants that have big, bold leaves, just to give a sense of scale and proportion.

I love to grow the umbrella plant for this reason. It has supersized leaves that look like they came right out of a jungle, but the plant itself can be very well behaved and it fits nicely into a border with other perennials, shrubs and trees.

Native to northwestern California and southwestern Oregon, *Darmera peltata* thrives in woodland areas beside streams. In my garden, I grow it on the east side of the house where it gets morning sun and afternoon shade.

In April, it produces superb flower stalks, which rise out of the ground and look very alien-like with tight, bright clusters of flowers formed at the end of short little stumpy stems. The moment this phase is over, the plant gets into serious foliage production, and by June, it has swallowed up a big chunk of space with its enormous, impressive leaves.

Being herbaceous, it dies down in fall, disappearing completely underground until the following spring when it rises to do it all over again. I find the whole cycle very uplifting.

Dicentra spectabilis

OLD-FASHIONED BLEEDINGHEART

→ There are three main types of dicentra: compact, fernleaf bleedinghearts, long-flowering fringed cultivars and the "old-fashioned" *Dicentra spectabilis* (old-fashioned bleedingheart). This last one is easily the most impressive.

It has lovely pink or white locket-shaped flowers that dangle like earrings from arching stems. Within this species, there is a rather novel cultivar called 'Gold Heart' that has yellow foliage and pink flowers. Peel away the outside of the flower and you will find a perfectly shaped Valentine's heart.

The Western bleedingheart (*D. formosa*) is native to the Pacific Northwest and has attractive, lacy foliage and produces flowers from late spring into summer. 'King of Hearts', 'Luxuriant', 'Langtrees' and 'Bacchanal' are all top cultivars, growing 8 to 10 inches (20 to 25 cm) high.

Fringed bleedinghearts (varieties of *D. eximia*) are also long-flowering and, like the fernleaf types, are a good choice for edging.

D. spectabilis is one of the first perennials out of the ground in spring but it is also immediately spotted by any passing slugs, so keep an eye on it to make sure it gets off to a good start.

After a wonderful show of flowers in April and May, plants will go dormant and die down by July, which can leave a hole in your shady border. The solution is to have a few pots of summer-flowering perennials such as astilbes or hostas on hand to plug the gap.

TYPE
perennial

SIZE
*2 to 3 feet
(60 to 90 cm)*

LOCATION
part shade

CONDITIONS
moist but well-drained soil

APRIL

Enkianthus campanulatus

PAGODA BUSH

TYPE
shrub

SIZE
*6 to 10 feet
(1.8 to 3 m)*

LOCATION
part shade

CONDITIONS
average, well-drained soil

➔ The flowers of enkianthus are the antithesis of the typically flamboyant modern hybrid rhododendron. The flowers of the pagoda bush, a shrub that is native to the mountains of Honshu in Japan, have a subtle sophistication due to their colour, diminutive size and habit of dangling in dense clusters. But they have loads of impact, abundant clusters of bell-shaped cream flowers with rose-pink veins and tips in spring. In full leaf, the bush forms an attractive, structurally useful green backdrop. In autumn, the small, oval-shaped leaves turn shades of crimson, yellow and orange.

It tends to be shunned by professional garden-makers mainly because of its low-key flowering habit and absence of colour in summer. It is, however, a treasured shrub, valued by true plant lovers.

'Red Bells' is a top cultivar, producing a bounty of bell-shaped flowers with red and pink veins in March and April and bright yellow, orange and red leaves in autumn. Also look for 'Albiflorus', a cultivar with creamy white flowers.

Locate it where the spring flowers can be easily seen and appreciated and where the exceptional fall colour can make a useful contribution. Enkianthus will grow in full sun provided it is rooted in moisture-retentive soil.

Erysimum 'Bowles Mauve'

PURPLE WALLFLOWER

→ With clusters of attractive pinkish purple flowers held above grey-green foliage, this shrubby perennial wallflower is a lovely addition for slightly warmer, sheltered gardens.

However, it is less hardy than most people think. It struggles in cooler gardens, but may possibly thrive in gardens that have a frost-free spot. In colder gardens, it needs to be replaced, although many gardeners (including me) vainly hope it will bounce back in spring full of vigour.

'Bowles Mauve' can fit nicely at the front of a perennial border or allowed to tumble over walls or slopes. It likes slightly alkaline soil, so add a little lime when planting.

Don't let flower stalks get too long. To promote bushy growth, pinch and cut back when flowering begins. If you want to try your hand at propagation, it is best to take softwood cuttings in early summer.

TYPE
perennial

SIZE
30 inches (75 cm)

LOCATION
full sun to part sun

CONDITIONS
sandy, well-drained soil

APRIL

TYPE
perennial

SIZE
*8 to 10 inches
(20 to 25 cm)*

LOCATION
light shade

CONDITIONS
average, well-drained soil

Geranium macrorrhizum

CRANESBILL, HARDY GERANIUM

➜ Cranesbills are real geraniums. The plants most people call "geraniums" are not geraniums at all, but *pelargoniums*. True geraniums are tough, winter-resistant plants with tiny, exquisite flowers that come in a delicious range of colours from sky blue to candy pink, royal purple to milk white. No garden should be without at least a couple of these outstanding, versatile plants.

Geranium macrorrhizum is a personal favourite. It is a compact, short plant with lovely magenta-pink flowers in spring. The foliage is also fragrant and evergreen in coastal gardens, which makes it a great ground cover. I use it everywhere—perhaps too much—to cover ground under trees and shrubs.

Other star performers include *G. cinereum* 'Ballerina', which has pink flowers with purple veins ('Lawrence Flatman' is almost identical), *G. cinereum* 'Pink Spice' with a low mound of purple foliage and pink flowers and *G. sanguineum* (blood geranium), which grows 6 to 10 inches (15 to 25 cm) high and has white, reddish purple or pinkish red flowers.

'Johnson's Blue' is an old favourite with sky-blue flowers in spring. 'Brookside' is another popular cultivar with blue-purple flowers, and 'Jolly Bee' has attractive blue flowers. But the best of the blues is 'Rozanne', which flowers profusely for a long period, from midsummer through to fall. They all grow between 18 and 24 inches (45 to 60 cm) high.

APRIL

Hosta 'Halcyon'

PLANTAIN LILY

→ Hostas are dependable, versatile and long-lasting. They are the workhorse plants of the perennial border. It is no surprise so many gardeners regard them as the perfect perennial. They come in an astonishing diversity of colour and form, but the blue-leaved varieties always strike me as the most attractive.

'Halcyon' is classified as a ground-cover type because it is low-growing and very manageable. Other great blues are 'Hadspen Blue', 'Blue Angel', 'Blue Dimples', 'Blue Wedgewood', 'Blue Moon', 'Blue Cadet' and 'Blue Boy'.

Best of the yellow-leaved varieties are 'Piedmont Gold', 'Sun Power', 'Midas Touch' and 'August Moon'. The biggest and boldest include such large-leaved cultivars as 'Sum and Substance', 'Krossa Regal' and 'Elegans'. For great green leaves, look for 'Devon Green' or 'Canadian Shield'.

For wonderful variegated foliage, there's no finer hosta than 'Frances Williams', an old favourite with pale-lavender flowers and heart-shaped, blue-green leaves trimmed with gold. Other fine variegated varieties include 'Francee', 'Frosted Jade', 'Great Expectations' and 'Minuteman'.

These all grow between 2 and 3 feet (60 to 90 cm) and thrive in light shade in moist, fertile soil.

TYPE
perennial

SIZE
12 to 16 inches (30 to 40 cm)

LOCATION
light shade

CONDITIONS
moist but well-drained soil

APRIL

Paeonia suffruticosa

TREE PEONY

TYPE
shrub

SIZE
*6 to 8 feet
(1.8 to 2.5 m)*

LOCATION
full sun to part shade

CONDITIONS
average, well-drained soil

→ Tree peonies are true shrubs with their permanent woody framework. They produce delicate, paper-thin flowers in spring in a wide range of colours from snowy white to pink to rich maroon. A mature specimen can produce hundreds of large blooms.

There are hundreds of types. Many are descendants of *Paeonia suffruticosa,* and they have wonderful poetic Japanese names that translate into titles such as "Coiled Dragon in the Mist Grasping a Purple Pearl."

There are dozens of modern cultivars, many with Chinese names. High-rated are 'Houki' (red), 'Feng Dan Bai' (white), 'Hu Hong' (pink), 'Wu Long Peng Seng' (purplish red) and 'Zhu Sha Lei' (soft pink).

They grow into substantial specimens, and some people put umbrellas over them to protect the fabulous flowers from being damaged by rain.

P. lutea has single, vivid-yellow flowers and attractive foliage. It grows to 6 feet (1.8 m).

Pelargonium citrosa

LEMON-SCENTED GERANIUM

→ Mosquitoes have become more than a nuisance with the advent of the West Nile virus, but you can drive these pesky insects away from your patio or deck and add a beautiful perfume to the air at the same time by growing a fragrant, lemon-scented geranium. *Pelargonium citrosa* (which, despite its common name, is a pelargonium and not a geranium) is often sold as the "mosquito plant" because the leaves contain a citronella scent that is supposed to repel the insect.

P. odoratissimum offers an apple fragrance while *P. tomentosum* has a discernible peppermint aroma. The Victorians liked to bring scented geraniums into the house in winter and place them where the leaves would be brushed by ladies' skirts as they walked by.

These plants also happen to be very drought tolerant, which means you can grow them in a pot without worrying too much if you forget to water them one day.

These are tender and must be moved to a frost-free place over winter. Ask about other scented geraniums at your garden centre. It is worth having a little collection of them.

TYPE
tender perennial

SIZE
2 feet (60 cm)

LOCATION
full sun

CONDITIONS
average, well-drained soil

APRIL

TYPE
shrub

SIZE
20 to 30 feet (6 to 9 m)

LOCATION
full sun to part shade

CONDITIONS
moist but well-drained soil

Phyllostachys nigra

BLACK-STEMMED BAMBOO

➔ Bamboo doesn't need to be a dirty word. It can be planted to create a privacy screen or grown in a container on a patio or deck for foliage interest.

Black-stemmed bamboo is a good choice because it has lovely glossy black canes and light, airy foliage and it is not invasive.

It is one of the most popular kinds used in China and Japan and one of the most sought-after by coastal gardeners because of its reputation for being less aggressive than other forms of *Phyllostachys*.

Other top-rated bamboos include *P. bambusoides* 'Castillonis Inversa', with green stems striped with yellow, and winter bamboo (*P. bissetii*), which is highly rated as a screening specimen with shiny, dark green culms and graceful, willowy foliage. These can both quickly grow 30 to 40 feet (9 to 12 m).

Clumping bamboo is desirable for obvious reasons: it doesn't run and is therefore not invasive. Popular clumpers include *Fargesia nitida*, *F. utilis* and *Chusquea culeou*, all of which grow 15 to 20 feet (4.5 to 6 m).

The secret to containing bamboo is to install a sturdy, seamless black plastic barrier at least 3 feet (90 cm) deep as the roots of bamboo never go deeper than 2 feet (60 cm). The barrier should be checked annually, and any rhizomes that are attempting to sneak over the top should be snapped off. A water course is also considered an effective barrier, but plastic containment is the recommended method.

APRIL

Polygonatum × hybridum

SOLOMON'S SEAL

→ While this is neither rare nor unusual,
Solomon's seal is one of the most loved perennials
for tucking under trees to create a full, lush
clump of attractive foliage on tall arching stems.
It also has delicate white flowers that add to its
architectural appeal.

Easy to grow, it is most at home in woodland
settings under trees and among shrubs with
hostas, bleedinghearts and ferns. It expands once
established. It can be divided easily every few
years in the fall, and unwanted clumps can be
passed on to friends.

Polygonatum odoratum 'Variegatum' is a cultivar
with variegated foliage—green leaves with ivory
edges—that has the same basic growth habit
and flowering characteristics but more than one
season of interest. 'Striatum' is a more uncommon
variegated form with creamy white streaks on its
green leaves.

Also check out *Smilacina racemosa* (false
Solomon seal), which resembles the foliage of
true Solomon's seal. It produces clusters of white
flowers at the end of the stems. It grows to 2 to 3
feet (60 to 90 cm).

TYPE
perennial

SIZE
3 feet (90 cm)

LOCATION
part shade

CONDITIONS
*moist but well-
drained soil*

APRIL

Primula bulleyana

CANDELABRA PRIMULA

TYPE
perennial

SIZE
*18 to 24 inches
(45 to 60 cm)*

LOCATION
light shade

CONDITIONS
moist soil

→ This elegant, architectural specimen with its lovely multiple tiers of flowers is perfect for planting alongside a creek bed, stream or pond. Native to China, it is considered by many to be the classiest member of the primrose family.

Primula beesiana is a close relative to *P. bulleyana;* some crossover between the two species has occurred.

Colours range from white, yellow and orange to apricot, pink and red. You can plant all these colours together, and they never seem jarring. In the garden, they require watering during drought days of summer because they are not tolerant of dry conditions.

Since they keep their leaves all year long, candelabra primulas usually need to be tidied up a bit in spring and all damaged foliage removed to make room for fresh new growth. Clumps can be divided anytime from September to April, although this is also best done in spring. Once established, the flowers freely seed themselves and eventually require thinning to stop them from becoming overcrowded.

APRIL

Primula vialii

CHINESE PAGODA PRIMROSE

→ Everyone falls in love with novelty primroses when they see them. They not only have great flowers, but they also promote conversation.

The Chinese pagoda primrose has short, pink, bottlebrush flower spikes with a distinctive red cone on top that makes it look rather like a miniature red-hot poker plant. It does self-seed, and if you get it in the right spot—a cool, well-drained, semi-shaded, woodland-type setting—you might have it for years to come.

Hybrids *Primula vulgaris* (page 59) and *P. × tommasinii* are called hose-in-hose primroses. They are novel little plants that produce two layers of flowers in shades of burgundy, rose, pink, white, yellow and red.

Their common name refers to a fashion style adopted by Elizabethan courtiers who wore two pairs of stockings, folding the outer pair to reveal the inner sock.

Hose-in-hose primroses are said to be among the world's oldest documented flowers. The earliest record of them is in John Gerard's book *Herbal*, published in 1597. 'You and Me' is a seed strain developed in the Czech Republic. Blooming from February to June, they grow to 12 inches (30 cm) high.

APRIL

Prunus serrulata

JAPANESE CHERRY

TYPE
tree

SIZE
25 and 30 feet
(7.5 to 9 m)

LOCATION
full sun to part shade

CONDITIONS
average, well-drained soil

→ If you are looking for a cherry tree that will bloom for you from mid- to late April and even into May, you will want to buy a cultivar of *Prunus serrulata*. These include 'Tai Haku' (the great white), 'Ukon' with pale creamy blooms, 'Shogetsu', which has pristine white flowers, and 'Kanzan', one of the most widely planted trees in Vancouver. 'Shirofugen' (the white goddess cherry) is one of the last to flower, producing beautiful pure white blooms in May.

Where space is tight, the columnar 'Amanogawa' could be the perfect fit. It has fragrant, pale pink flowers and is capable of rising straight up for at least 20 feet (6 m) and is rarely more than 3 or 4 feet (90 cm to 1.2 m) wide. Planted in a row, this tree can make a very good screen without taking up a lot of space with a bulky canopy.

The earliest flowering of the ornamental cherry trees are cultivars of *P. subhirtella,* blooming in autumn and again in late winter. The Yoshino cherry (*P.* × *yedoensis* 'Akebono', page 60) flowers in mid-March through to early April along with excellent cultivars like 'Accolade' (a cross between *P. sargentii* and *P. subhirtella*). Other popular varieties like 'Shirotae' (the Mount Fuji cherry) and 'Takasago' (a cultivar of *P.* × *sieboldii*) bloom from early to mid-April.

Pulmonaria
LUNGWORT

→ The spotted leaves of pulmonaria are thought to resemble the inside of a human lung. That's how it got its common name lungwort. But it is also known by many other names including soldiers and sailors, lords and ladies, Jerusalem cowslip, Bethlehem sage, spotted dog, Joseph and Mary, and Adam and Eve.

In early spring, the plant produces clusters of blue, pink or white flowers, which last for about three weeks.

Top cultivars are 'Dark Vader' and 'Trevi Fountain', both with blue flowers. 'Raspberry Ice' and 'Raspberry Splash' have pink flowers, while 'David Ward' has coral-pink blooms and 'Sissinghurst White' is a robust white form. There are dozens of others.

Older varieties have a bad reputation for powdery mildew. 'Mrs. Moon' is one to avoid since it is the least resistant to this fungal disease.

TYPE *perennial*

SIZE *8 to 10 inches (20 to 25 cm)*

LOCATION *part shade*

CONDITIONS *moist but well-drained soil*

Pyrus salicifolia 'Pendula'
WEEPING WILLOW-LEAVED PEAR

→ A lovely deciduous tree with silvery-grey leaves and a weeping shape, the weeping willow-leaved pear not only provides a striking contrast against dark green foliage, it can have a mesmerizing effect when the wind catches it and breathes life into its willowy branches.

In late spring, it has white flowers followed by small, inedible pears. It makes a good centrepiece in a border or a feature tree in a lawn. It can be evenly spaced to line an avenue and pruned into a graceful umbrella shape.

It was used by the celebrated English gardener Vita Sackville-West in her monochromatic white garden at the Sissinghurst garden in Kent, England.

Other similar cultivars are 'Silver Cascade' and 'Silfrozam' (Silver Frost).

TYPE *tree*

SIZE *20 feet (6 m)*

LOCATION *sun to light shade*

CONDITIONS *average, well-drained soil*

APRIL

Rhododendron augustinii

TYPE
shrub

SIZE
*5 to 8 feet
(1.5 to 2.5 m)*

LOCATION
full sun to part shade

CONDITIONS
average, well-drained soil

→ There are reasons rhododendrons are considered indispensable. They flower magnificently from early spring to midsummer. And they give the garden wonderful year-round structural integrity.

Best of the blue-flowering kinds is *Rhododendron augustinii*. It is without equal. At twilight, as other flowers start to recede into the night, its striking purplish blue flowers come to life with a luminous glow that remains until the last light of the day.

Other top blues, ranging from shades of purple to lavender blue, are 'Blue Diamond', 'Blue Peter', 'Blue Bird', 'Ilam Violet' and 'Susan'.

Other great rhodos, all flowering in April, include 'Etta Burrows' (red); 'Thor' (scarlet); *R. pseudochrysanthum* (pink-white blooms with a slight fragrance); 'Elizabeth' (bright red); 'Malahat' (red); 'Amoena' (azalea with vivid-magenta flowers that overlap with 'Blue Bird'); 'May Day' (orange-scarlet); 'Buketta' (dark red blooms); and 'Hello Dolly' (a blend of yellow, pink and peach with champagne-coloured indumentum on the undersides of the leaves).

TYPE
shrub

SIZE
6 to 10 feet (1.8 to 3 m)

LOCATION
full sun to part shade

CONDITIONS
average, well-drained soil

Ribes sanguineum

RED FLOWERING CURRANT

→ The red flowering currant is one of the best of all the native woodland plants in the Pacific Northwest. It is one of the first things hummingbirds look to feed from after their long flight back from wintering in Mexico.

It produces attractive clusters of red tubular flowers on erect branches from the end of March through April. The most popular cultivars are 'King Edward VII' and 'Pulborough Scarlet'.

While reasonably drought tolerant and mostly untroubled by pests and disease, it can become a target for aphids and can succumb to powdery mildew if starved of water and deprived of good air circulation during the hot days of summer.

This plant was not fully appreciated until it was reintroduced to Canada by the British. Plant-hunter Archibald Menzies is credited with having discovered it in 1793 when he came to BC with explorer Captain George Vancouver. The plant was taken to England, where garden-friendly cultivars (such as 'King Edward VII') were bred and popularized in the 1820s.

Other top names include 'Plenum', 'Spring Showers' and 'Elk River Red', an esteemed Oregon variety that can be found in many gardens in that state. 'White Icicle' is a relatively new cultivar developed at the University of BC Botanical Garden. It grows 6 to 8 feet (1.8 to 2.5 m), has lovely white flowers and is more shade tolerant than the red type.

The woodland garden is the most natural landscape for flowering currant, although it can be grown quite acceptably as a stand-alone feature specimen. Rhododendrons and azaleas are good companions, while hellebores, lungworts, heathers and spring-flowering bulbs are excellent choices for underplanting. Witch hazel will provide colour before *Ribes sanguineum* comes into bloom.

APRIL

Robinia pseudoacacia 'Frisia'

FALSE ACACIA, GOLDEN LOCUST

TYPE
tree

SIZE
40 feet (12 m)

LOCATION
full sun to light shade

CONDITIONS
average, well-drained soil

→ An exceptionally beautiful and graceful deciduous tree, *Robinia pseudoacacia* 'Frisia' is suitable for medium-sized and large gardens. Its bright, yellow-green leaves look even more sensational against the backdrop of dark brooding conifers.

You need plenty of open sky to grow it as its habit is to grow *up* rather than *out*. It can handle cold winters, being hardy to –20°F (–29°C), and doesn't mind hot summers since it is also reasonably drought tolerant. It manages to hang on to the fabulous colour of its foliage from the moment it leafs out in spring until the very cold days of fall.

If you like 'Frisia' you'll probably also like *Gleditsia triacanthos* 'Sunburst', known as the thornless honeylocust. It is a smaller, slower-growing tree with foliage that is distinctly frillier than 'Frisia'. 'Frisia' may have dramatic impact, but 'Sunburst' is easier to accommodate in the small- to medium-sized garden, growing 30 to 40 feet (9 to 12 m) in ten years. Two other popular cultivars of *Gleditsia* are 'Shademaster' and 'Skyline'.

APRIL

Tulipa

TULIP

→ Tulips look wonderful in big, open park spaces, but they can be problematic in the home garden. They need a very well-drained site, and they are often dug up and munched by squirrels. After tulips have finished flowering, the leaves can be large and messy and take up valuable space.

I prefer to grow mine mostly in pots, which can then be placed in the garden where they are needed for maximum impact in spring. When the flowers fade, I simply remove the pots.

Remember, early-flowering tulips are more likely to regenerate and come back year after year than ones that flower in late spring because they have more time to restore energy to the bulb before going dormant.

Those that have a better reputation than others for re-blooming year after year include 'Orange Trumpeter', an old favourite that is always high on the bestseller list. It blooms in April. Varieties of *Tulipa greigii,* such as 'Pinocchio' and 'Red Riding Hood', and cultivars of *T. kaufmanniana,* such as 'Chopin' and 'Heart's Delight', are also known as reliable re-bloomers.

TYPE
bulb

SIZE
*10 to 20 inches
(25 to 50 cm)*

LOCATION
full sun

CONDITIONS
average, well-drained soil

APRIL

continued on next page

(*Tulipa*, continued)

Other tulips known to return for a second and third year include 'Apeldoorn's Elite', 'Christmas Marvel', 'Couleur Cardinal', 'Don Quichotte', 'Golden Apeldoorn', 'Golden Melody', 'Orange Emperor' and 'Red Shine'.

Most reliable re-bloomers of all are the "botanical tulips." These are the species from which all the first hybrids were created. Look for *T. tarda* (bright yellow flowers), *T. clusiana* (red and white, candy-cane-type flowers), *T. chrysantha* (yellow-orange flowers), and *T. pulchella violacea* (purplish rose flowers). Especially popular are 'Lilac Wonder' (pale lilac petals and a yellow centre) and 'Eastern Star' (magenta-rose petals and a canary-yellow base).

Don't miss the opportunity to use tulips whether in the ground or in containers to add a little drama and fun to the garden. You'll get a big bang for your buck with high-impact hybrids such as the fringed, double and parrot tulips. 'Queen of the Night' and 'Black Diamond' are the two blackest tulips and have often been combined with red or white tulips to achieve a dynamic contrast.

Combination packs of "perfect partners" are available to take the guesswork out of planting. All you have to do is sink the bulbs into a pot and wait for the show to begin in spring.

All tulips are planted in the fall— mid-September to the end of October —6 to 8 inches (15 to 20 cm) deep in well-drained soil in a sunny spot.

Vinca minor

PERIWINKLE

→ While periwinkle is undoubtedly the most popular ground cover because of its glossy evergreen leaves and bright blue flowers, it also makes a very useful trailing plant for tucking into containers.

My favourite is the cultivar 'Illumination', which has bright golden-yellow leaves with a dark green edge. Like the common, plain-green *Vinca minor*, it also has blue flowers and has a habit of carpeting 2 to 3 feet (60 to 90 cm) wide.

However, it also looks very good when grown in a container, especially when combined with pineapple lilies (*Eucomis bicolor*) for an attractive summer display.

Periwinkle is mostly used to cover ground under trees and shrubs or as an edging plant along the side of paths. It is tolerant of dry shade once it is established, but during the first year after planting it is wise to water regularly.

Other notable cultivars include 'Atropurpurea' with purple flowers, 'Bowles' with intense blue flowers and 'Ralph Shugert' with light blue flowers.

TYPE
perennial

SIZE
4 to 6 inches (10 to 15 cm)

LOCATION
light shade

CONDITIONS
moist but well-drained soil

APRIL

MAY

TO-DO LIST

○ *Finish pruning forsythia, ribes and chaenomeles, cutting out dead, diseased and damaged wood and reducing shoots to strong buds or leafy side shoots.*

○ *Clean up rhododendrons and azaleas after flowering.*

○ *Pinch the tips of chrysanthemums and asters to promote bushiness.*

○ *Shop for annuals and other summer colour plants at the end of the month and plant them out after the risk of severe frost has passed.*

○ *Transplant half-hardy annual seedlings after the risk of frost has passed.*

○ *Plant tomato seedlings in a warm, dry sunny spot, ideally under an overhang or cloche to protect plants from excessive moisture. Try to make sure the planting spot is not one where you have had problems with tomato blight in the past.*

○ *Replace winter-flowering pansies, wallflowers and pot primulas with annuals and perennials.*

○ *Empty spring bulb containers and refill with summer colour plants.*

○ *Plant out dahlia tubers with a stake to support the mature plant.*

○ *Bring out tender exotics like brugmansia, fuchsia, lantana and tibouchina from the greenhouse.*

○ *Put out hanging baskets. Water daily and feed with half-strength 20-20-20 once a week.*

○ *Plant ornamental grasses, remembering that warm-season varieties like miscanthus and pennisetum will not start to grow vigorously until the soil is warmer.*

○ *Plant Brussels sprouts, bush beans, pole beans, pumpkin, squash and corn.*

○ *Mulch to suppress weeds, reduce evaporation and maintain soil moisture.*

○ *Clean up ponds and water features, and service pump and filters. Make sure water flow is still adequate for waterfalls and fountains.*

○ *Add new aquatic plants to your pond, such as water lilies, water lettuce and water hyacinth.*

MAY

Acer palmatum dissectum

LACELEAF JAPANESE MAPLE

TYPE
tree

SIZE
5 to 6 feet
(1.5 to 1.8 m)

LOCATION
part sun to light shade

CONDITIONS
average, well-drained soil

➔ More and more gardeners are creating colourful landscapes using foliage rather than flowers. Japanese maple trees are especially useful in this context for providing beautiful colour as well as great foliage texture in the garden.

The laceleaf maples are a wonderful low-growing type with finely cut, almost feathery, reddish purple or green foliage that cascades over twisted and contorted branches.

Top performers are 'Crimson Queen' (deep red) with orange-red to bright scarlet fall colour and its all-green cousin, 'Viridis'. Other highly rated cultivars are 'Inaba shidare' (purple-red), 'Red Dragon' (purple-red), 'Filigree' (pale green) and 'Seiryu' (more upright form, light green leaves).

Expect your laceleaf maple to grow quickly the first year. This is the time to make sure it develops a handsome overall shape and branch structure. Since the root system of Japanese maples is never very deep, it is important to keep your new tree well watered until it is established—don't let the ground around the tree become parched in the first year after planting.

Prune to enhance the tree's shape in the dormant season, when it has lost all its leaves. In late winter, before the sap starts to rise, judiciously prune again, taking away any dead, damaged and diseased branches.

MAY

TYPE
tree

SIZE
*15 to 20 feet
(4.5 to 6 m)*

LOCATION
part sun to light shade

CONDITIONS
average, well-drained soil

Acer pseudoplatanus 'Brilliantissimum'

SYCAMORE MAPLE

→ I love this slow-growing, lollipop-shaped tree for two reasons. First, it has outstanding shrimp-pink foliage in spring (a rival in my opinion to some cherries). And second, when that foliage turns green for summer, the tree still keeps producing bright patches of pinkish green leaves.

It is widely planted in British gardens. There is an entire grove of them at the famous Powis Castle garden in North Wales.

'Brilliantissimum' is best planted in a woodland setting where dark conifers or taller deciduous trees form a backdrop and protect the tree from having its leaves scorched by afternoon sun.

Three other quality maples with great foliage are *Acer shirasawanum* 'Aureum' (golden full moon maple), *A. negundo* 'Flamingo' and *A. platanoides* 'Drummondii' (Norway maple).

'Aureum' has tightly clustered, yellow-green leaves that can light up a corner of the garden. It, too, can scorch in direct sun, so it is best grown in light shade. It grows about 16 to 20 feet (5 to 6 m).

'Flamingo' has leaves with a flamingo-pink edge to them. The colour is even more pronounced in cooler areas where the tree's hardiness rating gets pushed to the limit. It grows to about 15 to 20 feet (4.5 to 6 m).

'Drummondii' has striking green leaves with wide, creamy white margins. It grows to 25 feet (7.5 m) in 20 years, eventually reaching a mature height of about 35 feet (10.5 m). It dislikes hot, dry sites.

MAY

Akebia quinata

CHOCOLATE VINE

TYPE
vine

SIZE
*20 to 25 feet
(6 to 7.5 m)*

LOCATION
full sun to part shade

CONDITIONS
average, well-drained soil

➜ If you want a vigorous vine that will cover an arbour, pergola or screening trellis and that not only has graceful foliage, but also chocolate-coloured flowers, *Akebia quinata* is the vine for you.

It is semi-evergreen in coastal gardens, and the flowers are a brownish claret-purple with a spicy, vanilla-like fragrance. They more than compensate for the vine's vigorous growth rate.

It grows by twining skinny tendrils around whatever it can get a grip on, so you need to provide a little support at the beginning. Train the vine where you want it to go, and once it is established you can simply concentrate on pruning it to shape. The roots don't like to be disturbed once they are settled. To keep your chocolate vine from taking off, prune it immediately after it has finished flowering in late spring.

The chocolate vine combines well with clematis and roses. Consider planting such roses as 'Albertine' or 'Francois Juranville' or a wine-red clematis like 'Madame Julia Correvon'. For chocolate-coloured flowers that also smell like chocolate, check out *Cosmos atrosanguineus.*

MAY

Allium aflatunense

ORNAMENTAL ONION

→ You won't find better value for your money than this classy bulb. It gives you great bang for your buck, producing a perfectly spherical purple ball of flowers atop a tall stem, and flowering from the end of May into June. It is my favourite of all the ornamental onions.

It is an ideal flower to generously scatter throughout a perennial border or to group together in a cluster as a main feature. In some gardens, it has been planted extensively under the yellow flowers of laburnum trees to achieve a particularly engaging contrast.

When the flowers fade, the flower heads are replaced by small, black seedheads that are almost as decorative.

When *Allium aflatunense* finishes flowering, *A. christophii* (Star of Persia, page 98) comes into bloom. It has an 8-inch (20 cm) globe of purple-silver star-shaped flowers. This is next followed by *A. aflatunense*'s bigger, bolder cousin, *A. giganteum*, which stands 4 feet tall (1.2 m) and has flower heads the size of a grapefruit.

Others to work into the garden include *A. caeruleum*, which has light blue flowers, *A. karataviense* with its pale purple globe-shaped flowers, *A. schubertii*, which has a spidery flower, *A. schoenoprasum* (chives) and *A. sphaerocephalon*, an elegant July-flowering drumstick type.

TYPE
bulb

SIZE
3 feet (90 cm)

LOCATION
full sun

CONDITIONS
average, well-drained soil

MAY

Allium christophii
ORNAMENTAL ONION, STAR OF PERSIA

→ It's a pity that most garden centres don't sell this in full bloom in May because whenever people see it they inevitably want to it for their garden. However, it grows from a bulb that needs to be planted in October, so people who see it in bloom for the first time are forced to wait a whole year before they can have a display of their own.

The magnificent 10-inch (25 cm) sphere of exquisite tiny, shiny star-shaped flowers is firmly held at the top of a tall sturdy stem. It is truly the star of the ornamental onions (alliums) and is a wonderful companion for ornamental grasses and heuchera.

If this is your first introduction to alliums, you will also want to have *Allium aflatunense* (page 97), with its neat purple ball of flowers at the top of a 32-inch (80 cm) stem, which blooms around the same time.

TYPE *bulb*

SIZE *12 to 15 inches (30 to 38 cm)*

LOCATION *full sun to part sun*

CONDITIONS *average, well-drained soil*

Araucaria araucana
MONKEY PUZZLE TREE

→ This spectacular evergreen has distinctive branches of sturdy, wedge-shaped leaves. It can reach more than 50 feet (15 m) in its lifetime, making a stunning sight.

The story goes that a group of gardeners had come across this tree in Cornwall, England, in 1850 when it was very rare in Europe (the tree is a native of Chile and Argentina). One of them commented that it would "puzzle a monkey to climb that"— and the name "monkey puzzle tree" was born.

Two other exotic trees for the coastal garden include the Tasmanian tree fern (*Dicksonia antarctica*, page 47), which has fabulous, long exotic fronds that stretch out from the top of a dark brown, hairy trunk, and the hardy banana *Musa basjoo* (page 110), which has the look of a typical desert island banana tree.

TYPE *tree*

SIZE *50 feet (15 m)*

LOCATION *full sun to part shade*

CONDITIONS *average, well-drained soil*

MAY

Astelia chathamica 'Silver Spear'

SILVER SPEAR ASTELIA

→ Once you begin to discover the beauty of ornamental grasses and other plants that are valued just for the beauty of their foliage, you will very quickly notice *Astelia* 'Silver Spear'.

It is native to New Zealand, where it has already become one of the favourite structural foliage plants in gardens, and it is considered an elegant challenger to the best of the cultivars of phormium (New Zealand flax grass), which is also very popular as a foliage plant.

'Silver Spear' gets its name from the silver-green colour of its swordlike foliage. It makes an ideal pot specimen. It is tender, which means it needs to be kept in a frost-free place over winter, but it is worth trying outside in the warmest, protected, California-like spots in your garden.

In my garden, I grow it in a large container with purple oxalis (*Oxalis regnellii* 'Atropurpurea') which bounces back every spring to provide a lovely colour and foliage contrast.

TYPE
perennial

SIZE
2 to 3 feet
(60 to 90 cm)

LOCATION
full sun to part shade

CONDITIONS
sandy, well-drained soil

MAY

Azalea 'Rosebud'

EVERGREEN AZALEA

TYPE
shrub

SIZE
*2 to 4 feet
(60 cm to 1.2 m)*

LOCATION
part sun to light shade

CONDITIONS
average, well-drained soil

→ All azaleas are rhododendrons, but not all rhododendrons are azaleas. In the early days of plant identification, they were thought to be two separate and distinct groups of plants, but as more research was done it was established that azaleas are actually members of the rhododendron genus.

'Rosebud' has lovely pink blooms that resemble miniature roses, which have been described as "wedding cake flowers."

Kurume hybrids are the most common evergreen azaleas. The most famous is 'Hino Crimson', which has vibrant crimson-red flowers and reddish foliage in the fall. All Kurume hybrids grow to about 18 inches (45 cm). Star performers include 'Hino Mayo' (rose-pink), 'Hino Orange' (apricot pink), 'Mother's Day' (dark red), 'Hinode Giri' (bright red), 'Avalanche' (white), 'Christmas Cheer' (bright red), 'Coral Bells' (coral red) and 'Blue Skies' (lavender pink). There are dozens more.

The Kaempferi azaleas grow to 4 feet (1.2 m). Top names are 'Johanna' (deep red), 'Othello' (coral red), 'Betty' (orange-red), 'Fedora' (medium pink), 'Blue Danube' (purple-red) and 'Dawn' (soft pink).

Girard azaleas are also highly rated. Look for 'Girard's Fuchsia' (reddish purple), 'Girard's Rose' (pink), 'Girard's Hot Shot' (brick red), 'Pink Dawn' (light pink), 'Aphrodite' (pink) and 'Geisha' (white).

Campanula

BELLFLOWER

→ Few flowers in the June garden command as much attention or look as cheery as the light sky-blue blooms of *Campanula persicifolia*. An old favourite of the English cottage garden, these lovely flowers make a great addition to the perennial border.

C. persicifolia is known as the peach-leaved bellflower. 'Alba' has dazzling white flowers with the same shape as the blue version. Other top cultivars are 'Chettle Charm' and 'Powder Puff'.

Other campanulas worth having in the garden include cultivars of the clustered bellflower (*C. glomerata*), which, like *C. persicifolia,* also looks great in the herbaceous border.

For rockeries and containers, there's the fairy thimble bellflower (*C. cochleariifolia*) as well as the low-mounding Serbian bellflower (*C. poscharskyana*) and Carpathian bellflower (*C. carpatica*).

Novelty kinds include 'Dickson's Gold', which has bright blue flowers and low-mounding golden-yellow leaves; 'Kent Belle' and 'Sarasota' with granny bonnet–type flowers; 'Kellys Gold' with bright chartreuse-yellow foliage, and 'Cherry Bells', 'Pink Chimes' and 'Bowl of Cherries', all of which are striking cultivars of *C. punctata*.

One of my favourites, and not always easy to find, is *C. latifolia* 'Alba', which has white, tubular, bonnet-shaped blooms.

TYPE
perennial

SIZE
*2.5 to 3 feet
(75 to 90 cm)*

LOCATION
full sun to part sun

CONDITIONS
moist but well-drained soil

MAY

Ceanothus impressus 'Victoria'

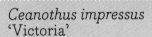

CALIFORNIA LILAC

➔ Native to California, ceanothus is a blue-flowering evergreen shrub that likes its summers warm and dry and its winters not too chilly. In full bloom from late spring to early summer, the blue flowers are a glorious sight.

'Victoria' is a good choice, which flowers profusely in early summer. It is a superior cultivar because it is compact and hardy enough to flourish in winter in a coastal garden without showing any cold damage.

Other top hybrids are 'Blue Mound' and 'Cascade'. Best of the deciduous varieties that flower later in summer are 'Gloire de Versailles' and 'Topaz', both of which sometimes put on a second flush of bloom in fall. For low-growing, carpeting types look for 'Blue Cushion', 'Hurricane Point' and 'Yankee Point'.

TYPE *shrub*

SIZE *10 feet (3 m)*

LOCATION *full sun to part shade*

CONDITIONS *average, well-drained soil*

Centranthus ruber

RED VALERIAN

➔ If you are keen to plant an old-fashioned cottage garden you'll want to work in a little red valerian, which produces fragrant, rose-red flowers for many weeks from midsummer on. It can bloom as early as May and continue through summer, re-blooming again in September.

Native to the Mediterranean region, it goes by an assortment of interesting common names including Jupiter's Beard and Spur Valerian.

It is a good pick for a hot, dry site in a drought-tolerant planting scheme. *Centranthus ruber* is the common species, but there is also a more compact cultivar called 'Coccineus'.

Although short-lived, red valerian does freely seed itself, and therefore once you have it in the perennial border, you are likely to have it year after year.

TYPE *perennial*

SIZE *15 to 24 inches (38 to 60 cm)*

LOCATION *full sun*

CONDITIONS *average, well-drained soil*

MAY

Choisya ternata

MEXICAN ORANGE BLOSSOM

→ With handsome evergreen foliage and fragrant clusters of white flowers, Mexican orange blossom is a first-rate shrub for growing in the garden but also in a container as well. This makes it an ideal plant for apartment or townhouse dwellers to grow on their deck or balcony.

Native to Mexico, it gets its common name also from the fact that the leaves give off a pleasant, fruity aroma when bruised and the white flowers have a slight citrus fragrance.

The best cultivar is 'Aztec Pearl,' although there is also 'Sundance', which has bright yellow leaves. Choisya is especially useful for foliage texture in the mixed border since the flowers only last for a few weeks.

If you like the smell of orange, you will probably also like mock orange *Philadelphus* (page 140), which produces white flowers that have a fruity, orangey fragrance.

TYPE *shrub*

SIZE *6 to 8 feet (1.8 to 2.5 m)*

LOCATION *full sun to part shade*

CONDITIONS *average, well-drained soil*

Clematis montana

ANEMONE CLEMATIS

→ For sheer spectacle, there are few plants that can deliver such a dramatic spring show as *Clematis montana*, a superb, vigorous, free-flowering vine from the Himalayas that produces loads of creamy white or clear pink flowers from mid- to late spring.

It can be grown into sturdy conifers or along fences to provide a huge splash of colour. To grow it into conifers, plant the vine a few feet away from the tree to allow the roots to get established and then train it over to the tree. It can also weave itself into the lattice of a trellis or crawl along the entire length of a pergola. It has also been successfully grown out of a pot and along the veranda of a house.

Top cultivars are 'Elizabeth', 'Alba', 'Fragrant Spring', 'Rubens', 'Pink Perfection', 'Tetarose' and 'Broughton Star'.

Flowers spring from old growth, so pruning should be done only after flowering to remove weak, damaged or diseased stems and for size and shape.

TYPE *vine*

SIZE *20 feet (6 m)*

LOCATION *full sun to part shade*

CONDITIONS *average, well-drained soil*

MAY

Cornus florida var. *rubra*
PINK-FLOWERING DOGWOOD

➜ Why choose a pink dogwood over a white one? Purists consider the white to be the perfect woodland specimen, but the pink has a charm of its own and can be equally spectacular.

A relatively fast-growing tree, *Cornus florida* var. *rubra* produces masses of soft pink flowers and prefers a warm, sheltered location that gets morning sun and shade in the afternoon. Good air circulation is important to prevent fungal diseases.

Top-named cultivars to look for are 'Sweetwater Red', which is thought to have the reddest flowers, and 'Cherokee Sunset'.

Other quality dogwoods to consider:

- *C. controversa* 'Variegata', which has bold, cream-white leaves that are held on tiered branches. This looks stunning against a dark background of conifers.
- *C. kousa* (Chinese dogwood), which has creamy white flowers. The excellent cultivar, 'Satomi', has pink flowers.

TYPE *tree*
SIZE *25 feet (7.5 m)*
LOCATION *full sun to part sun*
CONDITIONS *average, well-drained soil*

Digitalis purpurea
FOXGLOVE

➜ These majestic plants can be found in virtually every coastal garden—and every garden should have them. They seed freely, so once you have foxgloves, you will always have foxgloves. They look fantastic as they rise in spring to produce slender towers of superb flowers that are silky, tube-shaped and pinkish purple or white.

The most common are cultivars of *Digitalis purpurea,* such as the Excelsior hybrids and named varieties like 'Snow Thimble' (white), 'Silver Fox' (pink), 'Apricot Beauty' (apricot pink), 'Pink Champagne' (pink) and 'Primrose Carousel' (pale yellow).

It is also worth growing a few specialty foxgloves. Try *D. parviflora*, the Spanish foxglove, which has rusty-red flowers on sturdy stems and grows 30 to 40 inches (60 cm to 1 m) high, and the rusty foxglove, *D. ferruginea*, which has honey-brown flowers and grows exceptionally tall, from 4 to 6 feet (1.2 to 1.8 m).

D. × mertonensis is a shorter kind that grows to less than 3 feet (90 cm) and has deep copper-pink flowers.

TYPE *biennial*
SIZE *2.5 to 3 feet (75 to 90 cm)*
LOCATION *full sun to part shade*
CONDITIONS *moist but well-drained soil*

MAY

Erythronium

DOG'S TOOTH VIOLET

→ An easy-to-grow woodland plant, the dog's tooth violet has delicate, nodding, bell-shaped flowers that can be white, yellow, lavender or pale pink. It has been called the "soul of the spring" because of its exquite flowers, but it actually gets its common name from the dog-tooth shape of the tuberous bulb.

Erythronium revolutum is native to BC and the Pacific Northwest and has dark pink flowers, while *E. tuolumnense* is native to California and has golden-yellow flowers. 'Pagoda' is a popular yellow hybrid of these two. *E. dens-canis* originates from Europe and Asia and is the parent of great cultivars like 'Rose Queen'.

Although erythroniums have no disease and pest problems, they will fail to thrive if planted in soil that becomes too warm and dry during summer. They appreciate morning sunshine and afternoon shade. They look wonderful planted under trees or shrubs. The leaves disappear as summer progresses and the plant goes dormant.

TYPE
bulb

SIZE
12 to 16 inches (30 to 40 cm)

LOCATION
part sun to part shade

CONDITIONS
moist but well-drained soil

MAY

Euphorbia myrsinites

DONKEY TAIL SPURGE

→ The euphorbia family is one of the most talented in all of horticulture— it has several star performers. You ought to have at least two or three kinds in your garden. For the rock garden, gravel border, containers or over a sunny bank, *Euphorbia myrsinites* is an outstanding specimen with fabulous foliage and great flowers and very respectable resilience. (See page 31 for other great euphorbias.)

The elongated silvery-grey foliage has conelike scales (more reptilian than donkey tail–like to my eye) that make the plant very attractive all year round, even in the middle of winter. In spring, these stems produce lovely chartreuse flowers that last several weeks. Planted on the edge of a low retaining wall, the stems will tumble over in a most natural and elegant way.

When the flowers are finished, the plants needs to be tidied up with a little clipping. After that, it remains handsome all summer.

TYPE *perennial*

SIZE *6 inches (15 cm)*

LOCATION *full sun*

CONDITIONS *average, well-drained soil*

Hydrangea anomala subsp. *petiolaris*

CLIMBING HYDRANGEA

→ What a stunning climber this is! As well as having fantastic white lacecap-type flowers, it is such a vigorous vine, it can cover walls or fences or even grow high into conifers with little effort.

I grow two side by side in my garden to cover a wall that faces the neighbour's house on the west side. It gives the neighbour a beautiful sight in spring. By judicious and routine pruning, I am able to easily keep it under control and at the height I want.

It is self-supporting, climbing by means of tiny aerial roots that attach themselves firmly to any available surface.

The Japanese hydrangea vine, *Schizophragma hydrangeoides*, is a cousin and is just as vigorous. It has white flowers, but the petals are more spaced out. 'Moonlight' is a popular cultivar with green heart-shaped leaves with silvery veining.

TYPE *vine*

SIZE *30 to 40 feet (9 to 12 m)*

LOCATION *full sun to light shade*

CONDITIONS *average, well-drained soil*

MAY

Iris sibirica

SIBERIAN IRIS

→ There are more than two hundred species
and thousands of varieties of irises. It's easy to be
overwhelmed by the choices, but you will be more
than content growing a clump or two of Siberian
irises, a few bearded irises and some of the little,
early-spring-flowering irises.

The Siberian iris (*Iris sibirica*) has thin, upright
leaves and superb purple or blue flowers in May
and June. 'Silver Edge' has sky-blue petals that
have a distinctive silver edge. It is also considered
more vigorous than other hybrids.

Other top cultivars include 'Baby Sister' (bluish
mauve), 'Butter and Sugar' (creamy yellow),
'Caesar's Brother' (deep purple), 'Cambridge'
(light blue), 'Ewen' (purple with yellow markings),
'Sky Wings' (light blue), 'Papillon' (light blue) and
'Persimmon' (mid-blue).

Bearded irises have very solid, sword-shaped
leaves, and the flowers come in a remarkable
range of colours, from yellow, peach and pink to
blue, purple and black. They come in a range of
sizes from dwarf (less than 10 inches/25 cm) to
a standard tall (more than 28 inches/70 cm).
Look for 'Beverly Sills' (coral pink), 'Blue Staccato'
(bright blue with white edges), 'Cherub's Smile'
(pink) and 'Dusky Challenger' (black-purple).

TYPE
perennial

SIZE
3 feet (90 cm)

LOCATION
full sun to part shade

CONDITIONS
moist but well-drained soil

MAY

Kolkwitzia amabilis
BEAUTY BUSH

→ Native to central China, the beauty bush produces an avalanche of lovely small pink flowers with yellow throats. It is capable of growing to 16 feet (5 m) high by 8 feet (2.5 m) wide, but it can be kept down to a more manageable size with yearly pruning.

Through summer and into fall, it is mostly nondescript with plain dark green foliage, and being deciduous it loses all its leaves in winter. But when the flowers appear in April and May, it is one of the most sensational displays of the season.

The common species has white flowers, but the cultivar 'Pink Cloud' has the more desirable apple blossom–pink flowers.

A member of the honeysuckle family, the beauty bush reveals its connection in its arching branches and prolific flowering. However, kolkwitzia requires little pruning, perhaps a branch or two after blooming to maintain its compact shape. If you want to give a plant to a friend, take a cutting in July.

TYPE *shrub*

SIZE *16 feet (5 m)*

LOCATION *full sun to light shade*

CONDITIONS *average, well-drained soil*

Laburnum × watereri
VOSS'S LABURNUM, GOLDEN CHAIN TREE

→ One of the most exciting planting schemes was made world-famous by the late Rosemary Verey at Barnsley House in Gloucestershire. She took a spectacular avenue of golden-yellow laburnum and underscored the trees with the purple, spherical flower heads of countless alliums. This image has been reproduced in books and magazines all around the world.

The best of the laburnum trees is Voss's laburnum (*Laburnum × watereri*), hybridized in Holland at the end of the 1800s. This fast-growing tree can become 20 feet (6 m) high by 15 feet (4.5 m) wide. It produces drooping chains of bright yellow flowers that can measure up to 2 feet (60 cm) long. These have earned the tree its common name "golden chain tree."

Laburnum has been used in a variety of gardens to create fabulous avenues of late-spring colour. It is also a good specimen to use as a solitary tree to give special accent to the end of a garden or the centre of a lawn.

TYPE *tree*

SIZE *20 feet (6 m)*

LOCATION *full sun to part sun*

CONDITIONS *average, well-drained soil*

Magnolia 'Butterflies'

YELLOW MAGNOLIA

→ Not all yellow magnolias are created equal. Some are certainly better performers than others. But all yellow magnolias have one thing in common—they are all children of the cucumber tree, *Magnolia acuminata*, a native of eastern North America.

Today, there are as many as 40 kinds of yellow magnolia cultivars. People snap them up the moment they see them in bloom. August Kehr, of North Carolina, one of the world's most esteemed magnolia hybridizers, is responsible for developing some of the best.

Excellent cultivars are 'Butterflies', 'Elizabeth' and 'Yellow Bird', but also ask about less common hybrids such as 'Sunburst', 'Yellow Fever', 'Golden Endeavor', 'Sun Spire' and 'Gold Star'.

What differentiates them? Beauty is in the eye of the beholder, but magnolia experts say 'Yellow Bird' is "precocious" and tends to produce leaves too early, which obscures the flowers. The blooms of 'Elizabeth' are a paler, primrose yellow that tend to fade to cream in summer. 'Yellow Fever' gets high marks, but is criticized for having smaller flowers with a tinge of pink to them. 'Butterflies' is rated best of the lot because it produces flowers with a deeper, more durable yellow.

The Royal Horticultural Society has decided to sit on the fence saying that it is still too early to decide which is the best.

TYPE
tree

SIZE
20 feet (6 m)

LOCATION
full sun to light shade

CONDITIONS
moist but well-drained soil

MAY

Musa basjoo

HARDY BANANA

TYPE
tree

SIZE
12 to 18 feet
(3.5 to 5.5 m)

LOCATION
full sun

CONDITIONS
average, well-drained soil

→ Why grow a banana tree in your garden? Hmm, because gardeners in Toronto can't? No, the real reason we like to do it is that it gives the garden such a lush and tropical desert-island look.

Musa basjoo comes from the Ryukyu Islands of Japan. If it were simply left to go through a typical winter here, it would die down to the ground just like an herbaceous perennial and revive in spring.

However, most coastal gardeners want their tree to fit the classic desert-island image, so it is necessary to protect the trunk from cold in winter. This means wrapping the tree from the end of October to mid-April. With diligent care, hardy bananas can be grown to 16 or 18 feet (5 to 5.5 m) high. In very warm summers, they will even set fruit, although it is never good enough to eat.

TYPE
annual

SIZE
10 inches (25 cm)

LOCATION
full sun

CONDITIONS
average, well-drained soil

Nemesia fruticans 'Blue Bird'

NEMESIA

→ *Nemesia* 'Blue Bird' is one of the best annuals to give a garden colour and vitality in summer. Grown in hanging baskets or containers, it is a flawless performer. It's both heat and cold tolerant and has the ability to flower for months.

Top cultivars are all hybrids of *N. fruticans*. They include 'Compact Innocence' (white), 'Safari Pink', 'Safari Plum' and 'Safari White'. Also look for the Sunsatia series, which features several award winners.

Everyone has a favourite "summer colour" flower—petunias, marigolds, lobelia, impatiens, nicotiana, pelargoniums and so on. As well as nemesia, I also always make bold use of the following:

- *Diascia* (twinspur) is a perpetual bloomer that won't fizzle out as long as it is well watered. It is available in red, coral or pink. 'Red Ace' is the best known, but the Flying Colors series is highly rated.

- *Brachycome* (Swan River daisy) has both light, feathery green foliage and dainty pale blue, lavender or white flowers with yellow centres.
- *Calibrachoa* (million bells) has become the number one rival to petunias and is available in a range of colours including red, blue, pink, yellow, lavender and terracotta.
- *Bacopa* (sutera) that produce red as well as lilac flowers are available, although white is still the most popular.
- *Verbena* can be grown in a variety of locations. The new Superbenas have a vigorous growth habit, come in vivid colours and are exceptionally resistant to powdery mildew. 'Dark Blue' and 'Burgundy' are the top sellers. Cultivars in the Babylon series bloom earlier and have a more cascading habit, making it ideal for window boxes, troughs and hanging baskets.

MAY

TYPE
shrub

SIZE
4 feet (1.2 m)

LOCATION
full sun

CONDITIONS
moist but well-drained soil

Phormium

NEW ZEALAND FLAX

→ Nothing gives a garden a lush tropical look better than a few simple pots of phormium. If you have banana trees, bamboo and windmill palms in your garden, you will definitely want a few pots of phormium to complete the look. Use them to add colour and foliage texture on your patio or around your pool. These are easy-care plants that deliver a big bang for your buck.

Phormiums are available in a variety of beautiful colours from deep purple to neon pink to green with yellow stripes. They have upright, swordlike leaves that are long and elegant, and there is plenty of room under them in a pot to plant lobelia, bacopa, petunias or some other trailing summer colour plants.

They are only at risk when temperatures drop to 14°F (−10°C), which means they need to be brought into a frost-free environment in winter. In some gardens this is not a problem, and they can stay outside all winter.

The hardiest is *Phormium cookianum*, which in the ground can soar to 7 feet (2 m). However, this is not the most popular kind. Favourite cultivars include 'Atropurpureum', 'Yellow Wave', 'Sundowner', 'Flamingo', 'Dusty Chief' and 'Tricolor'. There are dozens more hybrids worth checking out.

Astelia chathamica 'Silver Spear' (page 99) also has the look of a phormium, but with attractive silver-green foliage. Like phormiums, it is also native to New Zealand. It grows 3 feet (90 cm) high in a pot and has excellent drought tolerance.

TYPE
shrub

SIZE
5 feet (1.5 m)

LOCATION
part sun to light shade

CONDITIONS
average, well-drained soil

Rhododendron yakushimanum

YAK RHODODENDRON

➜ It is hard to imagine a garden in the Pacific Northwest without rhododendrons. You don't have to have dozens of them, but it would be a mistake not to have a few.

You make an excellent choice when you pick *Rhododendron yakushimanum*, which is native to the Japanese island of Yakushima. It has deep pink buds that develop into compact, dome-shaped apple blossom–pink flowers. The tidy, elliptical leaves have the added interest of suede-like indumentum underneath.

This rhodo is a parent of many fine cultivars, including a series named after Disney's seven dwarfs. Colours range from pale yellow to white to soft pink. Names to look for are 'Ken Janeck', 'Renoir', 'Hoppy', 'Hydon Dawn', 'Rendezvous', 'Grumpy' and 'Dopey'.

All are slow-growing, but they eventually reach about 5 feet (1.5 m) and provide structural elegance in the garden. The species (the original plant and genetic parent of all these cultivars) is considered by many experts to be superior to any of the hybrids.

Other great rhodos that flower in May:
- 'Goldkrone' is much admired for its oval shape and glossy foliage. It produces yellow blooms.
- 'Gartendirektor Glocker' is one of the top German *williamsianum* hybrids. It produces dark rose flowers and has new foliage the colour of copper.
- 'Scintillation' has beautiful pastel-pink flowers with brown speckles and a lovely overall shape.
- 'Hyperion' has striking white flowers with a dark purple blotch.
- 'Vulcan's Flame' has red blooms.

MAY

Rodgersia aesculifolia

TYPE
perennial

SIZE
*3 to 4 feet
(90 cm to 1.2 m)*

LOCATION
part shade

CONDITIONS
*moist but well-
drained soil*

→ With fabulous big leaves that are coarse, crinkled and chestnut-like, plus amazing astilbe-like flowers, this is a spectacular perennial that can be grown in the woodland garden as a poolside plant or in a container as a special feature plant.

The leaves are so beautiful and architecturally stunning, it's easy to overlook the added bonus of the super flowers, which start out white and then turn a light shade of pink.

Rodgersia pinnata is similar, but its leaves are a little bigger and it is later blooming, with white to pale pink flowers. 'Superba' is a coveted pink-flowering cultivar. Its new foliage has a coppery tone to it. Less vigorous than its more common cousin the white-flowered rodgersia, 'Superba' is not always easy to find at garden centres and may require a dedicated search.

If you like rodgersia, you'll probably also like *Astilboides tabularis,* which has similar leaves and flowers and also likes moist soil. This herbaceous perennial is especially valued for the architectural beauty of its foliage. It grows 3 to 4 feet (90 cm to 1.2 m).

Syringa

LILAC

→ Lilac season comes and goes quickly, but gardens are wealthier for the abundance of heavenly scented, cone-shaped blooms.

The most popular kinds are the French lilacs, hybridized in the 1870s by French nurseryman Victor Lemoine. They grow 8 to 10 feet (2.5 to 3 m) and require minimal maintenance.

Cultivars bred by Russian hybridizer Leonid Kolesnikov are also reliable. The most famous is 'Beauty of Moscow', with pink buds that turn to white flowers with a frilly, dense, petalled look similar to noisette roses.

Top lilac cultivars include 'Edith Cavell' (cream), Madame Lemoine' (white), 'Decaisne' (purple), 'Miss Ellen Willmott' (white), 'Charles Joly' (magenta) and 'Belle de Nancy' (double pink). Also look for 'President Lincoln' (light blue), 'Sensation' (purple with white edge), and 'Andenken' and 'Ludwig Spath' (reddish purple).

A good mid-season blooming lilac is *Syringa* 'Miss Kim', a dwarf Korean lilac that grows about 6 to 8 feet (1.8 to 2.5 m) high and has fragrant clusters of icy purple flowers.

TYPE
shrub

SIZE
8 to 10 feet
(2.5 to 3 m)

LOCATION
full sun to light shade

CONDITIONS
average, well-drained soil

MAY

TYPE *shrub*

SIZE
8 to 10 feet (2.5 to 3 m)

LOCATION
sun to part shade

CONDITIONS
moist but well-drained soil

Viburnum plicatum var. *tomentosum* 'Summer Snowflake'
SUMMER SNOWFLAKE VIBURNUM

→ Most moderately sized gardens have room for at least two or three different kinds of viburnum. It is an extremely versatile family of shrubs, especially useful for providing ground cover or winter colour or fragrant white blooms in spring.

'Summer Snowflake', a plant introduced by the University of BC Botanical Garden, is ideal for a low-maintenance garden. It covers itself in April to May with a full flush of white, clover-shaped flowers. 'Summer Snowflake' has a compact form and slow-growing habit.

And if you have space, few shrubs are as spectacular as *Viburnum mariesii*. Its pure white, flat flowers are elegantly displayed along the entire length of its horizontal, tiered branches.

Other viburnum to look for:

- *V. × bodnantense* 'Dawn' has super-fragrant pink flowers on bare branches, which bring colour in January and February. It grows 8 to 10 feet high (2.5 to 3 m).
- *V. burkwoodii* (Burkwood viburnum) is an English hybrid that grows into a nicely rounded shrub 8 to 10 feet (2.5 to 3 m) high by about as wide.
- *V. opulus* 'Sterile' (also known as 'Roseum') is well known for its spectacular display in June of dazzling, creamy white, globular flower heads.
- *V. carlesii* (Korean spice viburnum) is an outstanding spring-flowering shrub that grows into a rounded 4 by 4 foot (1.2 by 1.2 m) bush with heavily scented white clusters of flowers in March and April.
- *V. davidii* is a first-rate ground cover that grows to 2 feet (60 cm). It has glossy evergreen leaves that are long and pointed and produces tiny metallic-blue berries. Its value has been somewhat diminished by overuse in the urban landscape, particularly in flower beds around shopping malls and gas stations. Nevertheless, it remains a great plant that can still serve a purpose in the home garden.

MAY

TYPE *vine*

SIZE
20 to 30 feet (6 to 9 m)

LOCATION
full sun to part shade

CONDITIONS
moist but well-drained soil

Wisteria floribunda

JAPANESE WISTERIA

→ It can be a heavenly experience to sit beneath an arbour or walk through a pergola smothered with the fragrant flowers of wisteria in May.

There are two popular types. *Wisteria sinensis* (Chinese wisteria) is particularly vigorous and produces soft-purple clusters that can measure up to 8 inches (20 cm) long. *W. floribunda* (Japanese wisteria) is slightly smaller and hardier.

While the pale purple and pink wisterias are beautiful, there is nothing quite like the pristine clarity of an all-white wisteria. This looks exceptionally classy in the garden, especially when underplanted with alliums and peonies.

W. floribunda 'Alba', which also goes under the names 'Snow Showers' and 'Longissima Alba', is the best pick. Other top Japanese wisterias are 'Kuchi-Beni', 'Macrobotrys', 'Multijuga' and 'Rosea'. Top Chinese varieties are 'Amethyst', 'Caroline' and 'Blue Sapphire'.

Grown from seed, wisteria is notorious for taking its time to flower. You will hear people warn that new plants can take as long as seven to ten years to bloom. But today most vines are grown from cuttings or grafting or layering. They are often in flower when you buy them in the pot at the nursery.

Although you will see spectacular photographs of wisteria in full bloom covering the brick facades of old Victorian houses, wisteria is not the best choice of climber to grow against a house. It can easily get out of hand, and the stems eventually become very woody and weighty. They can powerfully twist themselves around supporting structures and become a problem. Wisteria is much more suitable for growing along a sturdy pergola or over a sizable arbour. Think twice before growing one against the front of your house.

MAY

JUNE

TO-DO LIST

○ *Deadhead faded hellebores, remove old stems of pulmonaria (lungwort) and prune back spring-flowering euphorbias (Euphorbia polychroma and E. griffithii) by a third.*

○ *Clean up rhododendrons, kalmia, lilacs and azaleas after flowering.*

○ *Deadhead roses as well as annuals and perennials to promote more blooms.*

○ *Don't allow clematis to become tangled and unruly. Train it the way you want it to grow over an arch or against a trellis.*

- ○ *Carefully cut or pull up morning glory. You can stop it from becoming rampant by attacking it repeatedly.*
- ○ *Fill containers and planters with an assortment of summer-colour plants. Don't miss the opportunity to try New Zealand flax (Phormium) and purple fountain grass (Pennisetum setaceum 'Rubrum') in large pots and planters on your deck or patio.*
- ○ *Feed hanging baskets, petunias, fuchsias and pelargoniums with 20-20-20 liquid fertilizer weekly.*
- ○ *Prune early-blooming shrubs such as spirea, viburnum and lilac when they finish flowering. Start new plants by taking softwood cuttings from these shrubs.*
- ○ *Deal with aphids, slugs and other pests without resorting to pesticides. Hunt for slugs after rain or at night, and knock aphids to the ground using a jet of water from a hose.*
- ○ *Reduce clusters of apples to reduce weight on branches and promote big fruit later in summer.*
- ○ *Plant heat-loving vegetables such as peppers, cucumbers and eggplant.*
- ○ *Lift and divide congested clumps of irises once they have finished flowering. Replant rhizomes to form new colonies.*
- ○ *Sow sunflowers and other tender annuals.*
- ○ *Practice deep watering: water lawns and flower beds to get moisture deep into the soil, and then don't water again for a week.*

JUNE

TYPE
tree

SIZE
*16 to 25 feet
(5 to 7.5 m)*

LOCATION
sun to part shade

CONDITIONS
average, well-drained soil

Acer palmatum 'Bloodgood'

JAPANESE MAPLE

→ With its beautiful dark burgundy-red leaves and attractive blackish red bark, 'Bloodgood' is considered by many experts as the best of the upright red-leaved Japanese maples. It is the standard by which all others are judged.

What also makes it so praise-worthy is the fact that its leaves retain their beautiful colour all summer long compared to inferior clones that tend to have foliage that fades in the heat of summer.

You willl also come across 'Atropurpureum'. This is a name given to a wide variety of seedlings of *Acer palmatum*, all of which have red leaves.

Other top Japanese maples to consider:
- 'Fireglow' is similar to 'Bloodgood' but with brighter red foliage.
- 'Katsura' has leaves that turn from pale yellow with orange edges in spring to light green in summer and to bright yellow and orange in fall.
- 'Koto-no-ito' means "harp strings," in reference to the elegant shape of its green leaves.
- 'Oshio Beni' has bright red foliage that turns an even brighter shade of scarlet in fall.
- 'Osakazuki' is a famous and still popular cultivar with brownish red foliage that turns a spectacular crimson in fall.
- 'Sherwood Flame' has handsome, reddish purple, almost burgundy leaves.
- 'Butterfly' has blue-green leaves edged in creamy white.

Also look for 'Shishigashira' (the lion's mane or lion's head maple), 'Trompenburg' (noted for its vigour and slightly rolled red leaves) and 'Shojo shidare' (slender, deep purple-red leaves).

JUNE

Achillea

YARROW

→ For a hot, dry site, there are few plants that perform as flawlessly as yarrow. Thanks to extensive hybridizing, cultivars are available in a wide range of colours, from bright red and yellow to subtle shades of pink, lavender and purple.

In addition to the attractive umbel-shaped flower heads that appear to hover in the air, yarrow also has lacy, fernlike foliage that is held up on sturdy stems.

Many of the popular hardy hybrids were developed in Germany by crossing two attractive species *Achillea filipendulina* and *A. millefolium.*

Top cultivars are 'Paprika' (cherry red with a gold centre), 'Heidi' (pink), 'Red Beauty' (crimson), 'Anblo' (pale yellow), 'Terracotta' (salmon pink) 'Moonshine' (yellow) and 'Apple Blossom' (soft pink). Cultivars of *A. filipendulina* such as 'Gold Plate' and 'Cloth of Gold' can grow up to 6 feet (1.8 m) high.

TYPE *perennial*

SIZE *18 to 24 inches (45 to 60 cm)*

LOCATION *full sun*

CONDITIONS *sandy, well-drained soil*

Actinidia kolomikta

KOLOMIKTA VINE, ARCTIC BEAUTY KIWI

→ The heart-shaped leaves of *Actinidia kolomikta* are what make it so magical. In full sun the tips look like they have been dipped in raspberry juice.

It gets its common name Arctic beauty kiwi from its ability to endure intense cold.

In my garden, I grow it over an arbour with a clematis, a rose, a honeysuckle and a chocolate vine to provide shade and privacy for a sitting area. The actinidia holds its own very well against the other vines, and in addition to the great foliage it has dainty white flowers in spring.

Make sure you don't accidentally buy *A. kolomikta*'s rampant cousin *A. chinensis,* the Chinese gooseberry. This species is so vigorous it will clamber to 30 feet (9 m).

TYPE *vine*

SIZE *10 to 13 feet (3 to 4 m)*

LOCATION *full sun*

CONDITIONS *average, well-drained soil*

JUNE

Alchemilla mollis

LADY'S MANTLE

TYPE
perennial

SIZE
14 inches (35 cm)

LOCATION
full sun to part shade

CONDITIONS
average, well-drained soil

→ An all-time favourite cottage-garden perennial, lady's mantle is loved for the way its leaves hold raindrops like diamonds. It is also valued for the lime-green colour and frothy texture of its sprays of flowers, which first appear in June and last for several weeks. No garden should be without it.

While its performance is always predictable, lady's mantle can be used in a variety of ways—as a ground cover or container plant, or for foliage contrast. Its most popular use is as a mounding foliage plant for filling out the front of a perennial border or softening the straight edges of a path or walkway.

Alchemilla mollis is native to meadows and woodlands of eastern Europe and western Asia. It is one of the first perennials to bounce back to life in spring.

A. alpina (alpine lady's mantle) is a smaller, more compact rockery plant that grows 6 inches (15 cm) high and has tiny yellow-green flowers in summer. It's not as versatile as its cousin *A. mollis*, so show it more care and grow it in slightly moist, well-drained, fertile soil.

A. ellenbeckii is another species; it's perfect for growing in between stepping stones in light shade to part sun. It grows only 2 inches (5 cm) high.

JUNE

Astilbe

FALSE SPIREA

→ A great workhorse plant, astilbes have many fine qualities: they produce lovely plumes of white, pink or red flowers; they are one of the first perennials to surface in the spring, producing attractive foliage; they have great structure, holding flower stems erect with no need for staking; they are extremely disease and bug resistant; and they can be easily divided every few years to make new colonies.

The *Astilbe × arendsii* group has some fine cultivars such as 'Fanal' (red), 'Amethyst' (pink), 'Elizabeth Bloom' (blousy pink) and 'Snowdrift' (white).

To create a long sequence of blooms, select different varieties that bloom at different times—early summer, midsummer and late summer. Look for cultivars of Chinese astilbes (mostly *A. chinensis*) such as 'Superba' (purplish pink), 'Intermezzo' (salmon pink), 'Purple Candles' (magenta- purple) and 'Visions' (mauve-pink); star astilbes (*A. simplicifolia*) like 'Sprite' (pale pink), 'Hennie Graafland' (shell pink) and 'Bronze Elegance' (deep pink); and tall Japanese astilbes, hybrids of *A. thunbergii*, such as 'Moerheim's Glory' (soft pink) and 'Red Charm' (cherry red).

TYPE
perennial

SIZE
18 to 24 inches (45 to 60 cm)

LOCATION
full sun to part shade

CONDITIONS
moist but well-drained soil

JUNE

Astrantia major

MASTERWORT

TYPE
perennial

SIZE
30 inches (75 cm)

LOCATION
part sun to light shade

CONDITIONS
moist but well-drained soil

→ Knowledgeable gardeners love masterwort for the delicacy of its small, pincushion-shaped flowers. It is a perennial that is native to European woodlands, with a long history of use in English country gardens.

Common masterwort has elegant, greenish white flowers with light pink centres. There are some wonderful cultivars with red flowers such as 'Ruby Wedding', 'Rubra' and 'Hadspen Blood'.

'Shaggy' and 'Margery Fish' have larger, frillier white bracts while 'Sunningdale Variegated' is a collector's item with green and white foliage and soft pink flowers. Two others to keep an eye out for are 'Roma' (pink) and 'Claret' (dark red).

Astrantia may topple onto its neighbours especially after a heavy rainstorm, but while some see it as untidy, others regard this relaxed look as charming and natural. Stake it as new growth emerges in early spring if you want it to behave more formally.

Astrantia combines well with astilbe, lady's mantle, hosta, rodgersia, ligularia and ferns.

JUNE

TYPE
shrub

SIZE
4 to 6 feet
(1.2 to 1.8 m)

LOCATION
full sun to part shade

CONDITIONS
*moist but well-
drained soil*

Azalea

DECIDUOUS AZALEA

→ Unlike evergreen azaleas, these are tall and showier with brightly coloured flowers that appear in June and July. They make a great addition to the shrub border or can be placed among perennials.

Top cultivars are found in six key categories: Ghent hybrids, Knap Hill azaleas, Exbury azaleas, Mollis hybrids, Girard hybrids and Occidentale hybrids.

Ghent azaleas (original hybrids developed in Belgium in the 1800s) are lovely, but hard to find. Top names are 'Narcissiflora' (pale yellow), 'Coccinea Speciosa' (orange-red), 'Nancy Waterer' (bright yellow) and 'Norma' (orange-pink).

Knap Hill azaleas, hybridized by Anthony Waterer in the 1870s at his nursery, Knap Hill, in Surrey, England; include 'Knaphill Apricot', 'Knaphill Pink' and 'Knaphill Red'.

In the 1930s, Lionel de Rothschild produced his own strain of azaleas using Knap Hill seedlings at his Exbury estate in Hampshire. These are known worldwide as the Exbury or Rothschild hybrids. Most popular are 'Hotspur Red' (bright orange-red), 'Strawberry Ice' (pink with orange blotches), 'Klondyke' (orange), 'Gallipoli' (apricot pink), 'Satan' (red) and 'Gibraltar' (orange-red).

The Mollis types have larger clusters of flowers in shades of yellow, orange and pink. Star performers are 'Anthony Koster', 'Dr. M. Oosthoek' and 'J. C. van Tol'.

Key Girard hybrids are 'Yellow Pom Pom', 'Red Pom Pom', 'Pink Delight' and 'Crimson Tide'.

The Occidentale hybrids are among the most fragrant. Top cultivars are 'Alba Magnifica', 'Delicatissima' and 'Gloriosa' (all white with pink blush).

JUNE

Calycanthus floridus

CAROLINA ALLSPICE

Canna

CANNA LILY

→ A big, beautiful deciduous shrub, calycanthus produces maroon flowers all summer long that have a distinct red wine aroma. Its branches also have the slight scent of cinnamon.

It is hardy in coastal gardens and has been known to flower for six months, from spring right through to fall.

Named cultivars include 'Edith Wilder' and 'Michael Lindsey'. 'Athens' is a more unusual form with yellow fragrant flowers that bloom a little earlier.

Native to the woodlands of the southeastern US, calycanthus thrives on the banks of streams and does best in a lushly planted shrub border where the soil is moist but well drained. It suckers vigorously and should be pruned immediately after flowering to keep it in bounds.

TYPE *shrub*

SIZE *6 to 8 feet (1.8 to 2.5 m)*

LOCATION *full sun to light shade*

CONDITIONS *moist but well-drained soil*

→ Gardeners love exotic flowers, hot colours and lush, tropical jungle-like foliage. This probably explains why canna lilies—native to tropical parts of South and Central America—are so popular.

Cannas grow from a rhizome and can be planted indoors in a pot in March or April, and then transplanted into the garden in May.

Plants are admired for their large banana-leaf-like foliage, which can be green, bronze-burgundy, marbled or variegated with a stripe. The vibrant flower colours range from red, yellow and apricot to pink, peach and orange.

Top cultivars include 'City of Portland' (pink), 'Pretoria' (orange blooms and green, yellow and red variegated foliage), 'Wyoming' (orange-peach), 'The President' (red), 'Tropicana' (orange-and-green-striped foliage) and 'Bengal Tiger' (orange flowers and green-and-white-striped leaves).

TYPE *rhizome*

SIZE *30 to 40 inches (75 cm to 1 m)*

LOCATION *full sun*

CONDITIONS *moist but well-drained soil*

JUNE

Cardiocrinum giganteum

GIANT HIMALAYAN LILY

→ A real showstopper in any garden, the giant Himalayan lily is what you grow if you want to impress (or scare) the neighbours. It grows to 9 feet (2.7 m) tall and has 6-inch-long (15 cm) trumpet-shaped flowers, which are fragrant and pure white with red throats.

The heart-shaped leaves also live up to their name at a whopping 18 inches (45 cm) in length. Gardeners often leave the seed heads for decoration. In Britain, these beautiful dead parts of the lily have been sold at Christmas as artistic decorations.

Once the plant has flowered, the bulb dies but not before producing new offsets, which can take seven years to flower. By October, the papery seeds are ready to be blown to the ground in the wind. They germinate easily, but seedlings are vulnerable to slugs.

TYPE
bulb

SIZE
9 feet (2.7 m)

LOCATION
full sun to part shade

CONDITIONS
average, well-drained soil

JUNE

Cistus

ROCK ROSE

TYPE
shrub

SIZE
4 to 6 feet
(1.2 to 1.8 m)

LOCATION
full sun

CONDITIONS
sandy, well-drained soil

→ The rock rose produces spectacular white or pink flowers from June to July. Native to the Mediterranean and other temperate zones of Europe, they are the perfect seaside plant.

Cultivars are not very tolerant of wet, cold winters, so they virtually insist on well-drained soil and a little winter protection—they thrive on sunny slopes.

The most popular hybrids are *Cistus ladanifer, C. × dansereaui, C. laurifolius* and *C. × purpureus;* some top-named cultivars are 'Silver Pink', 'Peggy Sammons', 'Decumbens' and 'Jenkyn Place'. But most types sold at garden centres are simply labelled according to colour—white, pink with blotches or white with blotches.

The term "rock rose" also refers to cultivars of *Helianthemum,* but these have smaller flowers and grow less than 12 inches (30 cm) high, making them good plants for edging, for carpeting banks or for allowing to tumble over low-retaining walls.

JUNE

Clematis × 'Jackmanii'

JACKMAN CLEMATIS

Coreopsis verticillata 'Moonbeam'

THREADLEAF COREOPSIS, TICKSEED

→ There is a reason clematis is called the "Queen of Vines." It has incredibly beautiful flowers in a wide range of colours and types, and when well cared for clematis will perform flawlessly for years. No garden should be without at least two or three kinds. With almost two hundred varieties in commercial cultivation, there is no shortage of colours to choose from: 50 blue, 34 pink, 30 purple, 16 two-tone, 34 white, 21 red and 10 yellow.

'Jackmanii' is arguably the most reliable performer, producing masses of 4 to 6 inch (10 to 15 cm) purple flowers from June to August. Remember, the first year clematis sleeps, the next it creeps and the third year it leaps.

Plant clematis at least 18 inches (45 cm) deep, with its roots in the shade and foliage and flowers in full sun. Prune close to the ground in early spring and it will bounce back will full vigour. An easy-to-remember pruning rule for clematis: if it flowers before June, don't prune (or prune very carefully).

TYPE *vine*

SIZE *12 to 20 feet (3.5 to 6 m)*

LOCATION *full sun to part shade*

CONDITIONS *average, well-drained soil*

→ Yellow isn't everybody's favourite colour, but it is one of nature's. *Coreopsis verticillata* 'Moonbeam' is an exceptional plant with lovely yellow flowers and attractive lacy foliage.

It blooms prolifically from late spring into summer, producing hundreds of small pale-yellow flowers that make an excellent contrast against plants with purple foliage such as *Eupatorium* 'Chocolate' or *Physocarpus* 'Diablo'.

Other top cultivars of coreopsis are 'Golden Showers', 'Zagreb' and 'Early Sunrise'. Also check out 'Limerock Ruby' and 'Sweet Dreams', two striking hybrids of *C. rosea*. 'Sweet Dreams' has creamy pink flowers with a red eye and 'Limerock Ruby' has spectacular ruby-red flowers somewhat similar to chocolate cosmos. They both grow to about 2 feet (60 cm).

TYPE *perennial*

SIZE *12 to 18 inches (30 to 45 cm)*

LOCATION *full sun*

CONDITIONS *average, well-drained soil*

JUNE

Geranium × oxonianum

HARDY GERANIUM, CRANESBILL

TYPE
perennial

SIZE
*16 to 24 inches
(40 to 60 cm)*

LOCATION
full sun to part shade

CONDITIONS
*moist but well-
drained soil*

→ Every garden should have at least two or three different kinds of hardy geranium. They flower beautifully, they are disease and pest proof and they are easy to care for.

The *oxonianum* category is especially useful for providing masses of small, bright, colourful flowers all summer (from June to September).

There are at least 16 varieties available in the Lower Mainland. Flowers are mostly shades of pink, but there is plenty of variation in shade and veining.

Gerarium × oxonianum are indefatigable bloomers, continually stretching themselves to produce more flowers. Star performers are 'Phoebe Noble' (pink), 'Wargrave Pink', 'Claridge Druce' (pale pink) and 'A. T. Johnson' (blue).

The herbaceous border is the perfect home for any of these. Give them plenty of room to loosely intermingle with other perennials such as daylilies and astilbes, scabiosa and bee balm, phlox and lychnis.

Other sensational hardy geraniums worth knowing include 'Rozanne', 'Pink Spice', 'Ballerina', *G. sanguineum* and its cultivar 'Album'.

Gunnera manicata

GUNNERA

→ A bit of a monster plant, like something from a 1950s dinosaur movie, gunnera is loved for its stately and architectural presence and the sense of drama it brings to the landscape. This is all created by its massive rhubarb-like leaves.

Gunnera, which is native to Brazil, is often used as a feature plant next to lakes, ponds or streams, but it also thrives in the humble bog garden.

In the winter, its leaves can be cut and used to protect the growth buds around the crown of the plants from heavy frost.

The Chilean rhubarb (*Gunnera tinctoria*) is similar, and is often mistaken for the larger-leaved *G. manicata*.

Other big-leaved plants to consider for your garden include *Darmera peltata* (page 72), which produces quirky pink flowers before the large, rhubarb-like leaves appear; *Rheum palmatum* 'Atrosanguineum', which has large leaves and bright crimson flower plumes and the plume poppy (*Macleaya cordata*), which has grey-green leaves and can jump up to heights of 7 feet (2 m).

TYPE
perennial

SIZE
*8 to 10 feet
(2.5 to 3 m)*

LOCATION
full sun to part shade

CONDITIONS
moist, boggy soil

JUNE

Hebe buxifolia

SHRUBBY VERONICA, BOXLEAF HEBE

TYPE
shrub

SIZE
*3 to 4 feet
(90 cm to 1.2 m)*

LOCATION
full sun

CONDITIONS
average, well-drained soil

→ In early summer when *Hebe buxifolia* is covered in tiny white flowers, you might be fooled into thinking that the flowers are the plant's main feature. But this surprisingly hardy shrub is mostly valued for the beautiful texture of its foliage and its lovely round, mounding shape, which can give year-round structure.

H. pinguifolia 'Sutherlandii' is similar with grey-green foliage and white flowers but forms a much smaller mound, only 15 inches (38 cm) high. It is, nonetheless, very attractive.

Native to New Zealand, most hebes are too cold-sensitive to survive in Canadian gardens, but some other hebes worth growing in a container so they can be moved into winter quarters include 'Patty's Purple', which has similar foliage to *H. buxifolia* and lavender-purple flowers and 'Autumn Glory', which has dark green, semi-glossy evergreen leaves and violet-blue flowers. There is also a variegated form of *H. speciosa* with violet-purple flowers.

Helictotrichon sempervirens
BLUE OAT GRASS

Hydrangea macrophylla
MOPHEAD HYDRANGEA

→ Few ornamental grasses are as versatile or as easy to grow as blue oat grass.

'Sapphire Fountain' is a great cultivar. It has all sorts of winning characteristics: a fabulous mounding form and outstanding, intense silvery-blue blades on arching stalks that slowly turn to straw by the end of summer. In mild areas it is evergreen, which adds much-valued colour to the garden in winter.

Maintenance is the key to success with all ornamental grasses. Most need a good haircut in spring. Blue oat grass is no exception. Using your hand as a rake, pull away all the old, sand-coloured grass. Take the remaining grass in your hands as if it were a head of hair and cut it back. This will promote new growth and keep the clump healthy and tidy.

TYPE *ornamental grass*
SIZE *18 to 20 inches (45 to 50 cm)*
LOCATION *full sun*
CONDITIONS *average, well-drained soil*

→ The most common hydrangea grown in coastal gardens, the blue mophead is still the envy of gardeners in colder parts of Canada where it is far too tender to survive winter.

Popular cultivars are 'Altona', 'Nikko Blue', 'Hamburg', 'Europa' and 'Teller Blue' (which also goes by the names 'Blue Tit' and 'Blue Sky'). Good dwarf varieties are 'Winning Edge' and 'Pink Elf'.

In acidic soil, *Hydrangea macrophylla* flowers will be blue. In more alkaline soil, the flowers tend to turn shades of red and pink. The reason is that hydrangeas with blue flowers end up absorbing more aluminum than the ones with pink or red flowers. By liming liberally, you can raise the pH of the soil by making it harder for the hydrangea to take up aluminum. This turns the flowers red instead of blue.

TYPE *shrub*
SIZE *4 feet (1.2 m)*
LOCATION *part sun to light shade*
CONDITIONS *moist but well-drained soil*

JUNE

Kniphofia

RED-HOT POKER, TORCH LILY

TYPE
perennial

SIZE
3 feet (90 cm)

LOCATION
full sun

CONDITIONS
moist but well-drained soil

➜ An exotic, architectural plant, the red-hot poker gets its name from its yellow flowers with their bright red tips—resembling a poker just drawn from the fire. However, there are also pretty yellow and orange cultivars that do not have that characteristic, so the name is certainly not all-inclusive.

There are many good varieties. Some bloom in spring; others in mid- or late summer. With careful selection, it is possible to have flowers in more than one season.

Top cultivars are 'Royal Castle', 'Flamenco' and 'Alcazar'. Best of the all-yellows are 'Percy's Pride', 'Little Maid', 'Jenny Bloom' and 'Primrose Beauty'. The best orange cultivars are 'Shining Scepter' and 'Orange Torch'.

Keep an eye out for snails: they love to embed themselves in the heart of the thick leaves and then happily chomp holes in the flower stems.

Kniphofia caulescens is a rare find with thick, blue-green leaves and reddish-coral flower buds that open into pale yellow flowers. It blooms in midsummer, grows 3 to 4 feet (90 cm to 1.2 m) high and makes a handsome container plant.

Leycesteria formosa

HIMALAYAN HONEYSUCKLE

→ With beautiful, deep red bracts that dangle from tall stems full of lush heart-shaped leaves, Himalayan honeysuckle adds great colour and structure at the back of a perennial border.

After putting on a show of flowers in late summer, the plant produces small red berries.

It can make it through the winter in most coastal gardens, but can succumb during very wet winters with prolonged cold spells unless it is planted in a well-protected spot.

Leycesteria 'Golden Lanterns' has a higher hardiness rating. It has dark purple-red bracts and bright yellow foliage with reddish new growth. It is a little more compact, growing 3 to 5 feet (90 cm to 1.5 m).

TYPE *shrub*

SIZE *6 feet (1.8 m)*

LOCATION *full sun to light shade*

CONDITIONS *average, well-drained soil*

Magnolia sieboldii

OYAMA MAGNOLIA

→ One of the most beautiful of all magnolias, this is much loved by connoisseur gardeners for the purity of its small egg-shaped flowers with translucent petals that eventually open into an elegant, nodding cup-shape from May into June.

In the centre of the flower is a pink to rose-crimson circle of stamens that makes the blooms even more attractive.

The only drawback to *Magnolia seiboldii* is that it is not easy to place; it has a habit of growing as wide as it is tall, which can be 15 to 20 feet (4.5 to 6 m) at maturity.

M. sieboldii is native to China, Japan and Korea. It is an excellent choice for a woodland garden.

TYPE *tree*

SIZE *15 to 20 feet (4.5 to 6 m)*

LOCATION *part shade*

CONDITIONS *fertile, well-drained soil*

JUNE

TYPE
shrub

SIZE
3 feet (90 cm)

LOCATION
full sun to part sun

CONDITIONS
average, well-drained soil

Melianthus major

PEANUT BUTTER PLANT, HONEY BUSH

→ Some plants you want just for the fun of it. They are novelty specimens that keep dinner guests amused. And they can also inspire children by convincing them that perhaps plants and gardening aren't that dull and boring after all.

Melianthus major has beautiful, serrated, grey leaves that smell of peanut butter when you rub them. Grow it in a pot next to *Cosmos atrosanguineus*, which has maroon flowers that smell like chocolate, and you have a botanical candy bar.

You can take it one step further and add a pot of *Cassia didymobotrya*, which is called the "popcorn plant" because its leaves smell just like hot buttered popcorn.

All these plants grow less than 3 feet (90 cm) in a pot. The popcorn plant is grown as a patio tree while the peanut butter plant is more like a little bush. Chocolate cosmos is only about 18 inches (45 cm) high, but the flowers are held on long, thin stems that wave around 12 to 16 inches (30 to 40 cm) above the plant.

Complete your garden with a *Eucomis bicolor* (pineapple lily), which actually looks like a pineapple, throw in a few lemon-scented geraniums and perhaps a few scented mints (*Mentha*), and you have a fabulously fun "food" garden full of novelty and sensory pleasure.

In winter, *Melianthus major* needs to be brought into a frost-free environment as it is too tender for most coastal gardens in BC.

JUNE

TYPE
water plant

SIZE
6 inches (15 cm)

LOCATION
full sun

CONDITIONS
still water

Nymphaea
WATERLILY

→ If you live in an apartment with a small balcony or a townhouse with a tiny patio, you can still have a few water plants. You could start with a waterlily.

For a tub or trough water feature, consider a dwarf waterlily such as 'Helvola', 'Little Sue', 'Baby Red' or 'Snow Princess'.

A waterlily requires the same amount of sunshine as a rose does to bloom properly—at least six to eight hours a day. For small ponds, look for 'James Brydon', which has rose-red peony-like blooms. If you have less light, pick 'Masaniello' (light pink), 'Joey Tomocik' (canary yellow with speckled leaves), 'Virginalis' (pure white) or 'Lucida' (red).

To complete your mini water garden, add some oxygenators—plants that float on the surface or sink under the water and help to keep the water clean. Easy-to-find oxygenators are hornwort (*Ceratophyllum demersum*), parrot's feather (*Myriophyllum aquaticum*), Canadian pondweed (*Elodea canadensis*) and water violet (*Hottonia palustris*).

To eliminate the risk of your pond or tub garden becoming a breeding ground for mosquitoes, treat the water with a product containing *Bacillus thuringiensis.* It is harmless to humans, animals and plants but deadly to mosquito larvae. Or you could stock your water garden with "mosquito fish" (*Gambusia affinis*), which will eat mosquito larvae but are too small to be of interest to herons or raccoons.

JUNE

TYPE
perennial

SIZE
*3 to 4 feet
(90 cm to 1.2 m)*

LOCATION
full sun to part sun

CONDITIONS
average, well-drained soil

Paeonia lactiflora

GARDEN PEONY, JAPANESE PEONY

→ The hottest news in peonies in recent years is a series called the Itoh peonies—a group of cultivars developed by crossing tree peonies with common garden peonies.

Names to look for are 'Bartzella' (sulphur yellow), 'Going Bananas' (pale yellow), 'Julia Rose' (coral red), 'Morning Lilac' (purple) and 'Kopper Kettle' (coppery pink).

But the biggest-selling peonies, and arguably still the most beautiful, are varieties of the Japanese peony, *Paeonia lactiflora*. Even non-gardeners have little difficulty identifying them because of their large, fragrant flowers and their lush foliage.

My favourites are 'Sarah Bernhardt' (apple-blossom pink), 'Mother's Choice' (a knockout pristine white) and 'Red Charm', which has the most stunning dense ball of red petals surrounded by a looser collar of bigger guard petals.

'Bowl of Beauty' is a long-time favourite that produces a spectacular bowl of bright rose-pink petals with a creamy yellow centre. And 'Glowing Candles' is a pale pink Japanese peony with yellow stamens.

Others to look for include 'Leto' (pure white), 'Kukenu-Jishia' (light pink), 'White Sands' (white with a yellow centre) and 'Largo' (rose-pink petals around a golden yellow centre).

All peonies like some protection from the heat of the afternoon sun. Weak flowering is often due to roots being planted too deep or over-fertilization. Stems should be pruned away in fall to prevent disease problems.

JUNE

Papaver orientale

ORIENTAL POPPY

→ Delightfully flamboyant, Oriental poppies are arguably the best of the poppy family. Yes, even when taking into account the highly seductive Himalayan blue poppy (*Meconopsis betonicifoli*a), the ubiquitous orange California poppy and the lovely yellow Welsh poppy (*M. cambrica*).

Oriental poppies are easy to grow, come in a wide range of colours and have enormous, satiny flowers that can measure 6 inches (15 cm) across. Popular cultivars are mostly a cross between two species, *Papaver orientale* and *P. bracteatum*.

Star performers are 'Blackberry Queen' (white with a deep purple centre), 'Beauty of Livermere' (red with a dark centre), 'Carneum' (salmon pink with a black centre) and 'Patty's Plum' (a pale, papery grey-purple).

Early colour breakthroughs were achieved by British hybridizer Amos Perry, and some of the best cultivars bear his name, such as 'Perry's White'.

After flowering, the clumps of hairy leaves go dormant and often completely disappear by late summer. The best time to divide clumps is from August to September.

TYPE
perennial

SIZE
3 feet (90 cm)

LOCATION
full sun

CONDITIONS
average, well-drained soil

JUNE

Philadelphus

MOCK ORANGE

→ One of the best summer-flowering shrubs, mock orange produces a profusion of white flowers with a discernible orange-blossom fragrance from mid-June to July.

It can be grown as a deciduous hedge, although it is mostly used in a shrub border. Native to the western United States, Japan and Mexico, it is both wind and drought tolerant.

Philadelphus coronarius has lightly scented white blooms, 'Aureus' has yellow leaves and 'Nanus' is a dwarf version, growing only 4 feet (1.2 m) high.

Other named varieties include 'Virginal', which has been around more than a century, 'Beauclerk', which has white flowers with a purplish centre and 'Belle Etoile', a compact medium-size shrub for a smaller garden.

Philadelphus gives a garden a reliable continuity of flowers by connecting late-spring rhododendrons with midsummer blooming roses, lilies and perennials.

TYPE *shrub*

SIZE *10 to 12 feet (3 to 3.5 m)*

LOCATION *full sun to light shade*

CONDITIONS *average, well-drained soil*

Phlomis fruticosa

JERUSALEM SAGE

→ Visitors to my garden always love the handsome grey foliage of *Phlomis fruticosa*, but it also produces wonderful yellow flowers that resemble clusters of tiny bananas.

There is evidence that this plant has been grown in gardens around the Mediterranean for more than four hundred years. Although it is found growing wild in Italy, Greece and Turkey, it not found in Jerusalem, despite its common name.

It looks terrific most winters and is only disturbed by prolonged cold periods and heavy snows. I have grown it for ten years without a problem.

P. russeliana is the more widely grown type of Jerusalem sage. It has slightly sticky heart-shaped leaves and clusters of ball-shaped, creamy yellow flowers that appear in layers along the upright stems.

TYPE *shrub*

SIZE *3 to 4 feet (90 cm to 1.2 m)*

LOCATION *full sun*

CONDITIONS *sandy, well-drained soil*

JUNE

Potentilla fruticosa

POTENTILLA, CINQUEFOIL

→ Gardeners often want the impossible: a plant that flowers beautifully and perpetually yet requires minimal or no maintenance, has no pest or disease problems and grows less than 3 feet (90 cm) high. There is, of course, no perfect plant, but potentilla is about as good as it gets.

With the longest flowering period of any garden shrub, it pumps out yellow, orange, red, white or pink blooms (depending on the variety) from June through to September. It is immune to most pests and disease, and it thrives in sun or light shade in the poorest of soils.

Star cultivars are 'Goldfinger' (yellow), 'Abbotswood' (white), 'McKay's White' (creamy white), 'Pink Beauty' (pink), 'Princess' (light pink fading to white), 'Tangerine' (orange-yellow), 'Red Ace' (orange-red) and 'Royal Flush' (rose-pink).

Best of the reds is 'Red Robin'; which has fiery, brick-red flowers that hold their colour in full sun instead of turning orange as some red- and pink-flowering types have a tendency to do.

Potentilla fruticosa is a great foundation plant in an exposed rock garden or sunny mixed border. It thrives in full sun or light shade in average or poor sandy soil that is more alkaline than acidic.

TYPE
shrub

SIZE
30 to 36 inches (75 to 90 cm)

LOCATION
full sun to light shade

CONDITIONS
average, well-drained soil

JUNE

Rosa 'Ballerina'

BALLERINA ROSE

TYPE
shrub rose

SIZE
4 to 6 feet
(1.2 to 1.8 m)

LOCATION
full sun to part sun

CONDITIONS
fertile, well-drained soil

→ Bred in 1937, 'Ballerina' produces abundant clusters of tiny cup-shaped, musk-scented flowers that are light pink on the outside and white in the centre, which gives them the appearance of a ballerina's tutu.

Considered a shrub rose, 'Ballerina' matures into a compact bush that can become 3 to 5 feet (90 cm to 1.5 m) wide.

It can be successfully grown in a container and makes an attractive deciduous hedge or medium-sized privacy screen. I grow two of them to flank an arch covered with the climbing rose 'Blossomtime'.

Some other first-rate shrub roses:
- 'Hansa' is a medium-sized bushy rose with deep mauve to red blooms.
- 'Blanc Double de Coubert' is a tough French-bred *rugosa* that grows to 5 feet (1.5 m).
- 'The Fairy' has been popular ever since its introduction in 1932. It has dainty, rose-pink flowers that are displayed in clusters and grows to 2 feet (60 cm) high.

JUNE

Rosa 'Elina'

ELINA ROSE, PEAUDOUCE ROSE

→ 'Elina' is an unbeatable hybrid tea rose. Robust and vigorous, it is disease resistant and flowers more abundantly than most hybrid teas, producing lightly scented lemon-yellow blooms that are large and exquisite. They make excellent cut flowers.

Bred in Ireland, it was first introduced in 1984 and immediately began winning awards. It has been held up as a perfect example of what a hybrid tea should be: hardy, vigorous and beautiful.

It was originally called 'Peaudouce' (French for "soft skin"), which turned out to be a mistake—the breeders found the name didn't sell so it was changed. This rose has won numerous top awards and received a rating of 8.6 out of 10 from the American Rose Society.

TYPE *hybrid tea rose*

SIZE *40 inches (1 m)*

LOCATION *full sun to part sun*

CONDITIONS *fertile, well-drained soil*

Rosa 'Flower Carpet'

FLOWER CARPET ROSE

→ For roses that flower non-stop all summer you can't beat 'Flower Carpet'. But you have to make a sacrifice—fragrance. Some of the best roses have little or no scent, but they are relentless bloomers and give you colour all summer.

Introduced in 1991 as a perpetual bloomer, 'Flower Carpet' lives up to its billing and more. It comes in six colours—white, red, pink, apple blossom, coral and yellow. It is also totally disease resistant and can be used to create a small hedge.

The Meidiland landscapes roses, developed by the famous Meidiland nursery in France, are also noted for their exceptional blooming habit. 'Pink Meidiland' is one of the best with warm-pink flowers with a white eye, but the red and white versions are also very good. They grow to about 4 feet (1.2 m) high.

TYPE *shrub rose*

SIZE *3 to 4 feet (90 cm to 1.2 m)*

LOCATION *full sun*

CONDITIONS *fertile, well-drained soil*

JUNE

TYPE
floribunda rose

SIZE
*4 to 5 feet
(1.2 to 1.5 m)*

LOCATION
full sun

CONDITIONS
fertile, well-drained soil

Rosa 'Hot Cocoa'

HOT COCOA ROSE

→ There are hundreds of roses vying for your attention at garden centres. Some of them have better credentials than others, having been put to the test in trial gardens before being introduced to the market.

Tom Carruth of Weeks Roses in California has had remarkable success hybridizing a first-class collection of performance roses—floribundas, hybrid teas, climbers and grandifloras—each with a high degree of disease resistance. Nine of these quality hybrids have won the coveted All-America Selections award.

'Hot Cocoa' is one of the best of the floribunda group. It has a unique flower colour that has been described as "smoky chocolate orange."

Carruth's other winning floribundas include 'Scentimental' (red and white striped), 'Betty Boop,' (yellow and ivory with red edges) and 'Julia Child' (butter yellow).

His best climbers are 'Fourth of July' (red, white and yellow) and 'Night Owl' (dark purple), both of which grow 10 to 14 feet (3 to 4.5 m).

Best of his hybrid teas are 'Memorial Day' (orchid-pink hybrid tea) and 'Marilyn Monroe' (apricot).

Star performers in the grandiflora group are 'About Face' (golden orange), 'Wild Blue Yonder' (reddish purple) and 'Strike It Rich' (golden yellow).

JUNE

Rosa 'New Dawn'
NEW DAWN ROSE

Rosa 'Rambling Rector'
RAMBLING RECTOR ROSE

→ This is a terrific climbing rose, one of the best ever developed. It flowers beautifully year after year and is ideal for growing along a fence.

'New Dawn' comes with an impressive pedigree and produces an outstanding flush of slightly fragrant, shell-pink blooms in early June. Once the initial flush is over, flowers continue to appear sporadically throughout summer.

'Awakening' is a hybrid of 'New Dawn' and has pink flowers. It is being touted as superior to its parent because it produces more foliage and more flowers, but the jury is still out on that one.

Other top climbing roses are 'Altissimo' (red), 'Albertine' (pale coppery pink), 'Compassion' (pink), 'Felicite Perpetue' (creamy white), 'Francois Juranville' (pale pink) and 'Royal Sunset' (yellow apricot).

TYPE *climbing rose*
SIZE *15 to 20 feet (4.5 to 6 m)*
LOCATION *full sun*
CONDITIONS *fertile, well-drained soil*

→ Here's a chance to do something dramatic in your garden. Take this fabulous rose and train it all the way along a fence or up into sturdy conifers. When it produces its bright clusters of delightfully fragrant white flowers, the effect can be fantastic and unforgettable. It also has lovely red hips in fall.

It is a rampant and super-vigorous rose. I have grown it in my garden for more than ten years, and each year it gets better and better. It now grows 40 feet (12 m) high into pine trees, and when it blooms it becomes a great pillar of white. Sensational.

'Rambling Rector' loves sun and water and requires no fertilizing once established. Pruning is impossible once it gets up into the air, but for the first few years along a fence the side-shoots should be trimmed back immediately after flowering.

TYPE *rambling rose*
SIZE *20 to 30 feet (6 to 9 m)*
LOCATION *full sun*
CONDITIONS *fertile, well-drained soil*

JUNE

Sambucus nigra

ORNAMENTAL ELDER

TYPE
shrub

SIZE
*6 to 10 feet
(1.8 to 3 m)*

LOCATION
full sun

CONDITIONS
*moist but well-
drained soil*

→ When they hear "elderberry," most people think of homemade wine and possibly large, billowy, pinkish white flowers. But there are some spectacular dark-leaved elderberry cultivars that are absolutely stunning with superb foliage and lovely midsummer flowers.

'Black Beauty' was developed in England in 2000 and has outstanding glossy black leaves that offer a wonderful contrast in the shrub or perennial border. Brought to North America in 2004, this cultivar has become especially popular with gardeners in the Pacific Northwest.

'Black Lace' is similar to 'Black Beauty' (some would argue that it is even better) with its dark purple-black foliage that has a light lacy look to it.

Both of these cultivars have creamy pale-pink flowers at the end of June, followed by red berries that can either be used to make wine or jam or left for the birds.

If you like the flowers of sambucus, you might also like to check *Holodiscus discolor* (ocean spray). It grows 6 to 8 feet (1.8 to 2.5 m) high, likes sun to part shade and produces creamy panicles of tawny white, sweetly scented flowers in June.

Scabiosa columbaria 'Butterfly Blue'

DWARF PINCUSHION FLOWER

Styrax japonicus

JAPANESE SNOWBELL TREE

→ What makes 'Butterfly Blue' a must-have plant is its energetic and never-ending flower production. It just keeps blooming and blooming without being pumped full of fertilizer. It's easy to accommodate at the front of the perennial border or in containers.

'Pink Mist' is its sister plant. It performs just the same, but has delicate pink instead of soft blue pincushion-like flowers. 'Misty Butterflies' and 'Pink Lemonade' are two other popular low-growing kinds.

For a taller growing scabiosa, try a cultivar of *Scabiosa caucasica* such as 'Fama'. For a classy connoisseur scabiosa-like plant, there's *Knautia macedonica*, which has beautiful burgundy button flowers. 'Mars Midget' is similar but is much more compact, growing only 15 to 18 inches (38 to 45 cm) instead of 2 to 3 feet (60 to 90 cm).

TYPE *perennial*

SIZE *15 inches (38 cm)*

LOCATION *full sun*

CONDITIONS *average, well-drained soil*

→ There are two exceptionally good trees that bloom in June: the Chinese dogwood (*Cornus kousa*) with its masses of white bracts (pink if you have the cultivar 'Satomi'), and the Japanese snowbell tree, which has small bell-shaped white flowers with tiny yellow centres.

Both are excellent trees, but the styrax is superior in my opinion because its elegant shape and attractive foliage make the tree just as beautiful when it is not in flower.

Although it is ideal for a medium-sized garden, *Styrax japonicus* can also be grown very successfully in a container or in bush form in the shrub border.

Clusters of tiny, green, nutlike seeds eventually replace the faded flowers. The seed clusters are another charming characteristic. They eventually turn brown and drop to the ground.

'Emerald Pagoda' is a highly rated cultivar. If you prefer pink flowers, there's 'Pink Chimes'.

TYPE *tree*

SIZE *25 feet (7.5 m)*

LOCATION *full sun to part sun*

CONDITIONS *average, well-drained soil*

JUNE

Thymus

THYME

TYPE
herb

SIZE
*1 to 2 inches
(2.5 to 5 cm)*

LOCATION
full sun

CONDITIONS
average, well-drained soil

→ This low-growing, sweet-scented herb makes a great ground cover. It is ideal in sunny rockeries or for filling the crevices between paving stones. It can also be grown in pots with spring-flowering bulbs like yellow crocus and short blue iris.

Woolly thyme (*Thymus pseudolanuginosus*) is a good choice for squeezing between flagstones. It can even be used as a lawn substitute.

Lemon thyme (*T. × citriodorus*) gives off a powerful lemon scent when the leaves are brushed. Good cultivars are 'Gold Edge', 'Silver Queen', 'E. B. Anderson' and 'Doone Valley'.

Common thyme (*T. vulgaris*), also known as "cooking thyme," has aromatic grey-green leaves and tiny, pale lilac flowers in June.

Creeping mother of thyme, or wild thyme (*T. praecox*), grows 3 or 4 inches (7.5 to 10 cm) high, has purple, red or white flowers and spreads to form an attractive matlike covering. You sometimes find it in garden centres under the label *T. serpyllum*. Good cultivars are 'Purple Carpet', 'Coccineus' and 'Elfin'.

JUNE

Weigela florida 'Wine and Roses'

RED WEIGELA

→ It is easy to end up with a landscape full of colour in May but empty of interest in August and September. 'Wine and Roses' is part of the solution and offers more than one season of interest.

Deep purple leaves emerge in spring and mature to a softer, dark purplish green by autumn. When the bright pink flowers appear, they contrast strikingly with the purple foliage.

As a bonus, this low-maintenance, pest-free shrub attracts hummingbirds. They can't resist the sweet-scented clusters of foxglove-like flowers.

Other top cultivars include 'Bristol Ruby', 'Red Prince', 'White Knight', 'Victoria' and 'Pink Princess'. They all grow 4 to 5 feet (1.2 to 1.5 m) tall.

For something unusual, try 'Carnaval', which has red, pink and white flowers on the same bush. It grows 3 to 4 feet (90 cm to 1.2 m) and flowers in June.

Best of the variegated types is 'Variegata', which has green leaves with deep yellow edges. It has pink flowers in June and grows to 5 feet (1.5 m) high.

TYPE
shrub

SIZE
5 feet (1.5 m)

LOCATION
full sun to part shade

CONDITIONS
average, well-drained soil

JUNE

JULY

TO-DO LIST

- ○ *Prune wisteria (two months after flowering) by cutting side-shoots back to five or six buds, about six inches from the main branch.*
- ○ *Prune early-summer-flowering shrubs such as kolkwitzia (beauty bush), choisya (Mexican orange), enkianthus, philadelphus and magnolia.*
- ○ *Pinch and prune chrysanthemums to promote bushiness.*
- ○ *Take cuttings from pelargonium (geranium), senecio and lavender.*

- ○ Tidy up perennial beds by cutting back lilies, campanula, centaurea, irises and delphiniums as flowers fade.
- ○ Deadhead roses, cutting back to a five-leaf cluster to promote repeat blooming.
- ○ Continue to deadhead annuals and perennials to get maximum blooms.
- ○ Try "stopping" your dahlias, which means pinching off the tip to promote new growth; also try "disbudding," which means reducing the number of buds to produce big, more voluptuous blooms.
- ○ Start to harvest raspberries, rhubarb, cherries and strawberries. Early potatoes will also be almost ready to harvest. Sow a second crop of lettuce and radishes.
- ○ Collect seed from foxgloves for sowing in pots and seed trays. The new plants can be transplanted where you want them to bloom.
- ○ Water deeply and less often. Deep watering promotes more vigorous root systems, enabling lawns and plants to cope with hot, dry spells.
- ○ Water hanging baskets and patio container plants every morning. On exceptionally hot days, they will need a second watering in the afternoon.
- ○ Lightly fertilize plants, especially petunias, in containers and patio containers every few days.
- ○ Cut bouquets of flowers to bring indoors.

JULY

Abutilon × hybridum

CHINESE LANTERN

TYPE
shrub

SIZE
*4 to 6 feet
(1.2 to 1.8 m)*

LOCATION
part sun

CONDITIONS
average, well-drained soil

→ The easiest way to dress up a patio, deck or poolside in summer is to grow one of these fabulous little trees in a large container. The range of colours is impressive and these particular hybrids bloom non-stop.

Abutilons have maple-like foliage. They are called Chinese lanterns because of its papery bell-shaped lantern-like flowers. Top cultivars are 'Julia' (yellow), 'Marian' (orange) and 'Eric Lilac' (pink).

They are native to Brazil, and not hardy. In the fall you'll need to move the plant in its container into a frost-free environment with reasonably good light. In the spring you can bring the pot back outside. Give the plant a boost of 20-20-20 fertilizer and watch it take off on another blooming streak.

Also check out *Tibouchina urvilleana* 'Rich Blue Sun' (princess flower), the number one bestselling summer patio tree. It is also native to Brazil and has large velvety leaves and violet-purple saucer-shaped blooms.

Another terrific novelty patio tree I love to grow purely for the conversations it promotes is the popcorn plant (*Cassia didymobotrya*); its foliage smells like hot buttered popcorn and it has bright yellow flowers.

Acalypha pendula 'Firetail'

DWARF CHENILLE, KITTEN TAILS

→ It is a mystery why more people don't grow *Acalypha* 'Firetail' in containers and hanging baskets on sunny patios and balconies. It loves heat and will pump out lovely red tassel-shaped flowers that are fuzzy and as soft as velvet all summer long.

Acalypha has been enjoyed for years as a novelty plant in Europe. 'Firetail' is a more compact cultivar for containers.

I have grown it in the same pot for the last three years. Being tender, it needs to be brought into a frost-free environment over winter. In spring, all it needs is a sip of water enriched with 20-20-20 fertilizer to make it start blooming again.

Native to Cuba and Florida, 'Firetail' thrives in full sun, taking as much heat as summer can give it as long as it is watered daily.

TYPE *tender perennial*
SIZE *12 to 16 inches (30 to 40 cm)*
LOCATION *full sun*
CONDITIONS *average, well-drained soil*

Albizia julibrissin

SILK TREE, MIMOSA TREE

→ Native to China, the silk tree has gorgeous feathery fernlike foliage and fragrant pink flower tufts from June to September, and is a favourite with bumblebees. It thrives in heat but also wants moisture at its roots. It usually requires deep watering a few times during summer's hottest months.

It rarely leafs out before the end of May, so it is best planted in a spot where it does not dominate the garden in spring. When leafless, its branches can look rather dead and depressing, especially when everything else is bursting back to life.

Once it has new leaves, however, *Albizia julibrissin* is a magnificent spectacle, a worthy addition to any garden, with its lovely flowers and great foliage that provide style, texture and welcome dappled shade.

TYPE *tree*
SIZE *20 to 30 feet (6 to 9 m)*
LOCATION *full sun to part shade*
CONDITIONS *average, well-drained soil*

JULY

Buddleia davidii

BUTTERFLY BUSH

TYPE
shrub

SIZE
*10 to 12 feet
(3 to 3.5 m)*

LOCATION
full sun

CONDITIONS
average, well-drained soil

➜ One of the easiest deciduous shrubs to grow, buddleia produces loads of beautiful cone-shaped flowers from midsummer until frost. It is much loved for its ability to attract birds and butterflies to the garden.

Indifferent to poor soil, it thrives wherever you plant it, provided it gets plenty of sun and occasional watering. It needs to be pruned back hard every year at the end of winter to keep it a manageable size.

Top cultivars include 'Black Knight' (deep purple), 'Adonis Blue' (deep blue) and 'Dartmoor' (magenta). 'Harlequin' is a popular variety with creamy variegated foliage and reddish purple flowers. Exceptional white-flowered varieties are 'White Cloud', 'Peace', 'White Bouquet' and 'White Profusion'.

Also check out *Buddleia alternifolia,* called the "fountain butterfly bush" because it produces a cascade of arching branches bearing tightly knotted mauve flowers. With a little effort, it can be pruned into an attractive small tree.

July is a good time to check out the different kinds at the garden centre. It has recently been tagged as a problematically invasive species because of its free-seeding habit, so you may encounter pressure not to plant it. But it is still regarded as a first-class and long-time favourite shrub.

JULY

Calamagrostis × acutiflora 'Overdam'

FEATHER REED GRASS

Clematis 'Pamiat Serdtsa'

HERBACEOUS CLEMATIS

→ Even the faintest whisper of a summer breeze can make the handsome plumes of feather reed grass gently sway from side to side. Once you have experienced the soothing, relaxing effect for yourself, you won't hesitate to find a place for this grass in your garden.

It rises early in spring, remains evergreen most of the year in coastal gardens and sends up sturdy stems of feathery, buff-coloured plumes that last well into the fall.

The cultivar 'Karl Foerster' was voted Perennial of the Year in 2001 by the Perennial Plant Association in the US for its overall beauty, disease resistance and reliability.

'Overdam' is shorter at 3 to 4 feet (90 cm to 1.2 m), making it more suitable for small gardens and containers, plus it has attractive variegated green-and-white foliage.

TYPE *ornamental grass*

SIZE *5 to 6 feet (1.5 to 1.8 m)*

LOCATION *full sun*

CONDITIONS *moist but well-drained soil*

→ Some people have a hard time growing clematis. I always tell them they should try growing one of the hardy herbaceous clematis before they give up in frustration.

'Pamiat Serdtsa' is one of the best. It rises and falls with other herbaceous perennials such as hostas and bleedinghearts. It needs support as it has no clinging tentacles. You can use a wire or wooden pyramid support or a wire-spiral structure like a tomato cage.

Other herbaceous clematis to try include *Clematis recta purpurea* (white flowers with bronze foliage), *C. heracleifolia davidiana* (lavender blue) and one of the "prairie" clematis such as 'Chinook' (violet-blue), 'Savannah' (pink), 'Gazelle' (white) and 'Medley' (pink).

TYPE *vine*

SIZE *10 feet (3 m)*

LOCATION *full sun to part sun*

CONDITIONS *average, well-drained soil*

JULY

TYPE
perennial

SIZE
4 to 6 feet (1.2 to 1.8 m)

LOCATION
full sun

CONDITIONS
average, well-drained soil

Crocosmia 'Lucifer'
MONTBRETIA

→ It's great when flowers are an added bonus on a plant—a bonus because it already has such wonderful foliage. That's the story with crocosmia, a perennial that is native to South America. It has lovely, upthrusting sword-shaped foliage, somewhat similar to gladiolus (to which it is related). It produces red flowers that come on the scene in late summer, just when the garden is in need of a fresh splash of colour.

Many people still call crocosmia by its old-fashioned name montbretia, but crocosmia is technically correct.

The colour is not a true red; it has more orange in it than most plant labels show. The colour can clash quite badly with pink flowers such as the billowy panicles of phlox.

Grow crocosmia as an architectural focal point in the perennial border or as a solitary stand. It is often excluded from perennial books since it grows from corms and is therefore often lumped with bulbs and tuberous plants.

Other than 'Lucifer', top cultivars include 'Vulcan' (red), 'Jupiter' (orange), 'Bressingham Beacon' (orange-yellow blend), 'Emberglow' (orange-red) and 'Firebird' (orange).

There are some terrific yellow-flowered varieties such as 'Walberton Yellow', 'George Davidson', 'Jenny Bloom', 'Solfatare' and 'Rowallane Yellow'. 'George Davidson' is my favourite. It grows to 30 inches (75 cm) and is especially suitable for hot, well-drained sites in either full sun or part shade.

JULY

TYPE
perennial

SIZE
4 to 6 feet (1.2 to 1.8 m)

LOCATION
full sun to part sun

CONDITIONS
fertile, well-drained soil

Delphinium elatum hybrids

NEW MILLENNIUM DELPHINIUM

→ For the longest time, the best delphiniums were from the Pacific Giants series, with popular cultivars such as 'Black Knight' (dark blue), 'Galahad' (white), 'King Arthur' (purple), 'Guinevere' (lavender pink) and 'Cameliard' (lavender blue).

But over the years, the strain grew weak. Flowers became smaller and plants began to lose their overall vigour. Then, New Zealand nurseryman Terry Dowdeswell came along and produced a whole new breed called the New Millennium Delphiniums. These have turned out to be stronger, chunkier and more disease resistant with longer-lasting flowers.

These sturdier, superior delphiniums offer the same popular flower colours as the Pacific Giants, from light and dark blue to bright white and soft pink, but the flowers are larger with more petals and the plants are much more resistant to mildew and more tolerant of heat.

Most popular are 'Blushing Brides', 'Dusky Maidens', 'Green Twist', 'Innocence', 'Pagan Purples', 'Royal Aspirations' and 'Sunny Skies'. They all grow to 6 feet (1.8 m) in full sun, in moist, well-drained, fertile soil.

As heavy feeders, delphiniums need a high-nitrogen fertilizer or manure to get the best results. Young plants need to be protected from slugs in spring.

Cut off the flower heads when they are faded. This often promotes a second flush in late summer.

JULY

Escallonia

REDCLAWS

TYPE
shrub

SIZE
4 to 6 feet
(1.2 to 1.8 m)

LOCATION
full sun to part shade

CONDITIONS
average, well-drained soil

→ Since it is somewhat cold-sensitive, this lovely if thorny flowering shrub is most suited to the sunny seaside garden. It can tolerate wind and is not bothered by salty sea air. Its oval-shaped leaves are glossy and the bush produces small pink flowers.

'Apple Blossom' is considered one of the most reliable and hardiest varieties and is a favourite with many gardeners. It gets its name from its dainty pink and white flowers, but it has a habit of becoming very twiggy and unkempt unless pruned regularly. Some gardeners actually like the wild, natural look, and never prune it.

It is one of several cultivars developed by the Slieve Donard Nursery in North Ireland. Other top performers from this nursery include 'Pride of Donard' and 'Donard Scarlet'.

Other reliable cultivars to look for are 'Peach Blossom', 'Red Hedger' and 'Pink Princess'. 'Newport Dwarf' is a shorter variety that grows only 18 to 24 inches (45 to 60 cm) high while 'Gold Brian' has golden foliage.

TYPE
shrub

SIZE
4 feet (1.2 m)

LOCATION
full sun to part shade

CONDITIONS
moist but well-drained soil

Fuchsia magellanica

HARDY FUCHSIA

→ Most people know fuchsias as the large, tropical-looking red and purple flowers they see trailing from hanging baskets or window boxes or trained into little patio trees grown in containers.

But the hardy varieties, natives of Chile and Argentina, can be planted and grown in the garden. They have beautiful red, slender, lantern-like flowers suspended from arching stems.

In the warmer West Country part of England, hardy fuchsias have been used to make hedges. In gardens here in the Pacific Northwest, they are mostly used as feature plants.

Fuchsia magellanica is the most reliable species. The slim flowers are red on the outside and purple inside. The two top performers are 'Gracilis' and 'Riccartonii'. They die down every winter and regenerate in spring.

Other forms to check out include the maiden's blush fuchsia (*F. molinae* 'Alba'), which, contrary to its name, has pale lavender-pink, not white, flowers and 'Aurea', which has yellow-green leaves and red and purple flowers.

Some other fuchsias will survive in sunny, sheltered spots in coastal gardens once they have established a good root system. They key to success is to grow them in containers until they have a decent root system and then transplant them into the ground in late spring. The Northwest Fuchsia Society lists dozens of varieties that it says have been "tested outdoors all year for three years on the West Coast of the Pacific Northwest."

Hemerocallis 'Stella de Oro'

DAYLILY

TYPE
perennial

SIZE
*12 to 15 inches
(30 to 38 cm)*

LOCATION
full sun to light shade

CONDITIONS
*moist but well-
drained soil*

→ One of the earliest daylilies to bloom and one that keeps on blooming the longest, 'Stella de Oro' is admired for both its lightly ruffled golden-yellow trumpet-shaped flowers and for its compact growth habit. Like all daylilies, it has lush green straplike foliage that forms an attractive mound.

Daylilies have been massively over-hybridized over the past few decades. There now exists an exhausting diversity of colour variations. Not all of them are top notch.

Some of the best include 'Catherine Woodbury', a classic with fragrant, pale pink blooms and a lime-green throat, 'Pardon Me' with cranberry-red petals and a yellow throat as well as the cultivars in the Trophytaker series.

Every year the American Hemerocallis Society polls its members to see what they rate as the best new cultivars. 'Ruby Spider', 'Ed Brown', 'Strawberry Candy' and 'Primal Scream' have been regular winners.

Hydrangea serrata 'Bluebird'

LACECAP HYDRANGEA

→ Called the "queen of flowering shrubs," hydrangeas are an indispensable component of the coastal garden.

Most popular are mopheads with their large, globular flower heads (page 133), and lacecaps, which have more decorative flower heads—dense centres skirted by a light garland of single flat flowers that resemble a scullery maid's hat.

Outstanding is 'Bluebird', which has striking blue lacecap flowers from the end of June to September. 'Blue Wave' is similar, but harder to find. Other popular lacecaps are 'Lanarth White' and 'Seafoam'.

Although hydrangeas will grow in full sun, the leaves often end up being scorched and start to look scruffy when overexposed to direct afternoon sun.

TYPE *shrub*

SIZE *4 to 6 feet (1.2 to 1.8 m)*

LOCATION *part sun to light shade*

CONDITIONS *moist but well-drained soil*

Kirengeshoma palmata

YELLOW WAXBELLS

→ An excellent plant for cool woodland gardens, kirengeshoma is considered a choice specimen, almost a collector's item, by plant connoisseurs. It is native to the woods and hillsides of Korea and the Japanese islands of Shikoku and Kyushu.

It has large, sycamore-shaped leaves and waxy, bell-shaped yellow flowers from July to October that hang down from purplish stems.

It is the perfect partner for other woodland plants such as bleedinghearts and corydalis, but it also thrives very well with hostas, candelabra primulas, rogersia and irises in soil that retains moisture in summer.

Kirengeshoma koreana is hard to tell apart from *K. palmata* to which it is so similar, but the flowers of *K. koreana* are a paler yellow and the plant itself is slightly larger.

TYPE *perennial*

SIZE *4 to 5 feet (1.2 to 1.5 m)*

LOCATION *part sun to light shade*

CONDITIONS *moist but well-drained soil*

JULY

TYPE
perennial

SIZE
2 to 3 feet
(60 to 90 cm)

LOCATION
full sun

CONDITIONS
average, well-drained soil

Lavandula angustifolia
ENGLISH LAVENDER, COMMON LAVENDER

→ One of the world's favourite herbs, lavender has been a mainstay in gardens for as long as gardens have existed.

Its primary scent is located in the dense clusters of tiny light blue or purple flowers, which are tightly bound together at the top of short, slender stems.

There are more than 28 species. The best cultivars are hybrids of *Lavandula angustifolia* such as 'Hidcote', which has bluish purple flowers on long, tumbling stalks and 'Munstead', which has bright violet-blue flowers.

'Sarah' is similar to 'Munstead', but grows a little taller and has larger flowers. 'Loddon Pink', 'Hidcote Pink' and 'Jean Davies' (a.k.a. 'Rosea') are pink varieties.

To keep your lavender tidy, clip the flower stalks as soon as the blooms start to fade. In spring, before buds break, give the plant a close haircut, but don't cut into old wood.

Specialty lavenders that are best grown in containers:

- *L. dentata* (French lavender) has grey-green foliage and fragrant, mauve-lavender flowers. It is tender and needs to be brought indoors in winter. It grows 2 to 3 feet (60 to 90 cm) tall.
- *L. stoechas* (Spanish lavender) has small, violet, butterfly-like petals at the top of deeper purple, pineapple-shaped flowers. It is a lovely plant to grow in a pot but needs to overwinter in a frost-free place.

Lavatera 'Barnsley'

TREE MALLOW

→ For sheer flower power, 'Barnsley' is unbeatable. It blooms virtually non-stop, producing attractive pink hollyhock-like flowers with a dark red centre from July to September. It brings a cheerful and relaxed old-world cottage-garden look to the summer border.

'Barnsley' gets its name from Barnsley House, the home and garden of one of Britain's most respected garden experts, Rosemary Verey. She lived in Gloucester, England, and died in 2002. 'Baby Barnsley' is a more compact form, growing only 4 feet (1.2 m) high and producing pink blooms with a bright pink centre.

Other popular kinds include 'Bredon Springs', 'Candy Floss', 'Ice Cool' and 'Kew Rose'.

Lavatera trimestris is an annual mallow that also flowers prolifically. Well-known hybrids are 'Mont Blanc' (pure white) and 'Silver Cup' (bright pink). Both grow 2 feet (60 cm) high and provide long-lasting colour.

TYPE
shrub

SIZE
*5 to 6 feet
(1.6 to 1.8 m)*

LOCATION
full sun to part sun

CONDITIONS
average, well-drained soil

JULY

Leucanthemum × superbum

SHASTA DAISY

TYPE
perennial

SIZE
*3 to 4 feet
(90 cm to 1.2 m)*

LOCATION
full sun to part sun

CONDITIONS
average, well-drained soil

→ American horticulturist Luther Burbank named leucanthemum the "Shasta daisy" back in the early 1900s because the white flowers reminded him of snow on Mount Shasta in California.

This universally loved daisy has since become a fixture of the herbaceous border, producing masses of white flowers, mostly with a yellow centre, from mid-July through to August.

It used to be called *Chrysanthemum maximum,* but went through a name change some years ago and is now known as *Leucanthemum × superbum.*

'Alaska' is the bestseller, while 'Becky' was named Perennial of the Year by the Perennial Plant Association in 2003. 'Snowcap' is also popular since it is more compact, growing to only 14 inches (35 cm) high. It is also more heat tolerant, which allows it to flower longer into summer.

Other top Shasta daisies include 'Sunny Side Up' and 'Broadway Lights'.

They all thrive in full sun or part shade in moist but well-drained soils, and need to be divided every two or three years to maintain vigour.

Liatris spicata

BLAZING STAR, GAYFEATHER

→ Trends in gardening tend to go in cycles. A plant that is popular today falls out of favour tomorrow. Liatris was once hugely popular, but people grew tired of it and stopped planting it. Now it seems to be gaining attention again, and people are making room for it in the garden.

It has slender, poker-like purple flower spikes, and grows in ordinary, moist but well-drained soil.

'Kobold' is the best cultivar. It grows a little shorter than the common species, rising only 2 feet (60 cm), which means the flower spikes are less lightly to topple over. This is a good variety for a drought-tolerant, water-wise garden. 'Floristan Violett's' also has purple flowers, but is taller, growing 3 feet (90 cm) high.

The cultivars that are commercially grown for cut flowers are 'Kobold' and 'Floristan White'; the latter has white flowers instead of purple and is very drought tolerant.

TYPE
perennial

SIZE
*2 to 3 feet
(60 to 90 cm)*

LOCATION
full sun to part shade

CONDITIONS
moist but well-drained soil

JULY

Lilium Asiatic hybrids

LILY

TYPE
bulb

SIZE
*3 to 4 feet
(90 cm to 1.2 m)*

LOCATION
full sun to part sun

CONDITIONS
moist but well-drained soil

→ Midsummer is the time when many gardeners kick themselves for not having taken more time in spring to plant lily bulbs. In July, the great procession of lily blooms begins in earnest and gardens everywhere begin to boast the most glorious lilies.

Asiatic lilies are the first to appear, coming into bloom at the end of June. Stars include names like 'Lollypop', 'America', 'Renoir' and 'Pink Pixie'.

In containers, lilies in the compact Pixie series offer splashes of bright colour, while those in the Kiss series ('Aphrodite', 'Fata Morgana' and 'Sphinx') are pollen free, making them more appealing to allergy sufferers who want to grow lilies in pots in close quarters on a patio or balcony.

As the Asiatic hybrids start to fade, the procession continues with Turk's cap lilies (*Lilium martagon*), tiger lilies, and trumpet lilies like 'Pink Perfection', 'African Queen' and *L. regale*. These are followed in August by super *L. martagon,* and fragrant Oriental lilies like the pure white 'Casa Blanca' and bright pink 'Stargazer'.

Lilium species

TURK'S CAP LILY

Magnolia grandiflora

SOUTHERN MAGNOLIA

→ This graceful style of lily gets its common name from its profoundly recurved sepals, which look swept back like a "Turk's cap." The species, *Lilium martagon*, is one of the most popular kinds and is the parent of many hybrids. It has medium-pink petals with black speckles and blooms from July to August.

L. superbum (the American lily) and *L. henryi* are similar with orange recurving petals and distinctive black speckles. Other popular species with the typical Turk's cap characteristic include *L. michauxii* (the Carolina lily) and *L. pardalinum* (the leopard lily).

Turk's cap lilies comes in a range of colours including pink, rose, mauve, magenta and white. Many have black spots which sometimes cause them to be mistaken for tiger lilies. As well as the swept-back petals, the flowers of turk's cap lilies usually have a green star at the centre, another distinguishing feature.

All of these lilies should be planted in fall or early spring for spectacular displays in midsummer.

TYPE *bulb*

SIZE *3 to 4 feet (90 cm to 1.2 m)*

LOCATION *full sun to part sun*

CONDITIONS *moist but well-drained soil*

→ If you like the look of a tropical-style garden with bamboo and banana trees, eucalyptus and ginger lilies, brugmansia and bougainvillea, you will probably be interested in the southern magnolia.

It has fragrant white bowl-shaped flowers with lemon-yellow centres that bloom in July, measuring as much as 12 inches (30 cm) across on a mature tree. The glossy evergreen leaves also have an attractive orange-brown soft down on the undersides.

Native to the southeastern US, it is better known in Florida and Carolina as "bull bay." In the Pacific Northwest, it can be vulnerable to cold winters and should therefore be planted in a sunny, well-drained, sheltered site.

Top cultivars include 'Victoria' (the most cold-tolerant), 'D. D. Blancher' and 'St. Mary'. 'Majestic Beauty' and 'Russet' grow taller, reaching 30 to 50 feet (9 to 15 m) at maturity.

For smaller gardens, 'Little Gem' is the best pick. It grows only 13 to 20 feet (4 to 6 m).

TYPE *tree*

SIZE *20 feet (6 m)*

LOCATION *full sun to part sun*

CONDITIONS *average, well-drained soil*

JULY

Monarda

BEE BALM, BERGAMOT

→ Bee balm injects colour and vitality into the garden in July and August with its bright red, candy pink or purplish blue flowers, which sit at the top of tall sturdy, stems.

This flower is a work of art, formed by more than a dozen smaller, open-throated, tubular flowers that look like snapping (or singing) crocodiles.

A mature clump of bee balm looks fantastic, especially contrasted with other eye-catching summer-flowering perennials like shasta daisies, phlox and lavatera.

Top names are 'Gardenview Scarlet', 'Marshall's Delight', 'Cambridge Scarlet', 'Scorpion', 'Croftway Pink' and 'Prairie Night'.

To prevent powdery mildew, make sure plants are not crowded (to prevent poor air circulation) and are well watered at their roots during hot spells.

TYPE *perennial*
SIZE *3 to 4 feet (90 cm to 1.2 m)*
LOCATION *full sun to light shade*
CONDITIONS *moist but well-drained soil*

Oenothera fruticosa

SUNDROPS

→ Once established, oenothera is drought tolerant, making it an ideal plant for growing in well-drained, sunny areas. It provides a riot of bright yellow or pink flowers from early summer on.

Most are cultivars of *Oenothera fruticosa*, a species native to eastern North America. Top varieties are 'Spring Gold', 'Fireworks' and 'Cold Crick'.

Other sundrops such as 'Sunset Boulevard' and 'Lemon Sunset' are cultivars of *O. versicolor*. These grow well in containers.

O. macrocarpa (Ozark sundrops) has fragrant yellow flowers and grows only 6 inches (15 cm) high.

The traditional showy evening primrose, *O. speciosa*, is especially vigorous and floriferous, with flowers that start out white and fade to pink. An excellent cultivar of *O. speciosa* is 'Siskiyou Pink', which has soft pink flowers.

TYPE *perennial*
SIZE *12 to 16 inches (30 to 40 cm)*
LOCATION *full sun to part sun*
CONDITIONS *average well-drained soil*

Persicaria amplexicaulis

MOUNTAIN FLEECEFLOWER

→ What can you grow alongside ornamental grasses? Rudbeckia and echinacea are popular picks, but for a big bushy partnership there's nothing like *Persicaria amplexicaulis,* which produces masses of pink or crimson flowers.

This perennial also works well with purple-leaved shrubs like *Physocarpus* 'Diablo' or the dark-leaved *Sambucus* 'Black Lace' or 'Black Beauty'.

The two best cultivars of mountain fleeceflower are 'Firetail' and 'Taurus'. Clumps can be divided in spring.

Also look for *Persicaria bistorta* 'Superba', which flowers earlier in May, grows 24 to 30 inches (60 to 75 cm) high and has pink bottlebrush flowers that look great when combined with the purple spherical flowers of *Allium aflatunense* (page 97).

Dwarf fleeceflower, *P. affinis* 'Dimity', is another winner. It makes a great ground cover or front-of-border edging plant and deserves to be grown in more gardens. It has red and pink flowers on short spikes about 8 to 10 inches (20 to 25 cm) high and forms a thick carpet of lush green leaves.

P. 'Painter's Palette' is admired for the unique pink, white and green variegation of its leaves. It grows 18 inches (45 cm) high and prefers part shade, which makes it a great plant for mixing under and around trees and shrubs.

TYPE
perennial

SIZE
3 feet (90 cm)

LOCATION
full sun

CONDITIONS
moist but well-drained soil

JULY

Phlox paniculata

GARDEN PHLOX

TYPE
perennial

SIZE
4 feet (1.2 m)

LOCATION
full sun to part shade

CONDITIONS
average, well-drained soil

→ *Phlox* is Latin for "flame," and *Phlox paniculata* sets the garden on fire with its bright, cheerful colours at the height of summer. This is a plant that gives you an exuberant, flamboyant look that expresses the fullness and abundance of summer at its peak. Colours range from hot pink and deep red to brilliant white and mauve-purple.

Mildew can be a problem, but it can be prevented by providing good air circulation and by watering well (to the roots) in the drought days of summer.

Most popular are 'Bright Eyes' (pink with a red eye), 'Fujiyama' (white), 'Orange Perfection' (salmon orange), 'David' (fragrant white) and 'Starfire' (red).

'Eva Cullum' (clear pink with a maroon eye), 'Franz Schubert' (lilac) and 'Sandra' (cherry red) are more compact varieties that grow only 2 feet (60 cm) high. 'Pinafore Pink' is one of the shortest, rising only 18 inches (45 cm).

Other cultivars include 'Nora Leigh' (white) and 'Harlequin' (purple), which have variegated green and white leaves. The most mildew-resistant hybrids are 'David' and 'Eva Cullum'.

Potentilla hybrids

CINQUEFOIL

→ Cousins to the woody, bushlike shrubby potentilla, these perennial non-shrubby cinquefoils grow into attractive, carpeting mounds of flowers.

The leaves are crinkled like those of a strawberry plant, and the flowers are cup-shaped and come in an assortment of colours including pink, red, yellow and orange.

Potentilla atrosanguinea has blood-red flowers above a rosette of strawberry-like, trifoliate green leaves. It grows to 20 inches (50 cm).

P. × hopwoodiana is considered the most sophisticated by some experts. It has pale pink heart-shaped petals that turn raspberry red at the centre.

P. nepalensis, the largest of the herbaceous potentillas, has top cultivars such as 'Miss Willmott' (crimson) and 'Helen Jane' (pink).

P. megalantha (woolly cinquefoil) has felty leaves covered with silvery hairs and bright yellow flowers.

P. × tonguei has apricot flowers with red centres. It is a good plant for late-summer colour and for growing at the front of the border.

TYPE
perennial

SIZE
*6 to 20 inches
(15 to 50 cm)*

LOCATION
full sun

CONDITIONS
average, well-drained soil

JULY

Rosa 'Graham Thomas'

ENGLISH SHRUB ROSE

TYPE
shrub rose

SIZE
4 feet (1.2 m)

LOCATION
full sun

CONDITIONS
fertile, well-drained soil

→ English roses were developed by Warwickshire rose-breeder David Austin by crossing some of the best old garden roses (ones that existed before the advent of the first hybrid tea, 'La France', in 1867) with the best modern roses.

His idea was to combine the grace and charm of antique roses with the repeat-blooming habit of top hybrid teas and floribundas. Not all of Austin's roses are brilliant, but 'Graham Thomas' certainly is.

Introduced at the Chelsea Flower Show in 1983, it has turned out to be a reliable performer, noted for its vigorous growth and the ability to generate glorious flowers throughout the summer. It won the prestigious Royal Horticultural Society Award of Garden Merit in 1993. It has superb golden-yellow cup-shaped blooms with a strong fragrance.

Other highly rated English roses include 'Gertrude Jekyll' (deep pink), 'Mary Rose' (pink), 'Winchester Cathedral' (white), 'Shropshire Lass' (pink), 'Leander' (apricot) and 'Constance Spry' (pink).

JULY

TYPE
shrub

SIZE
*18 to 24 inches
(45 to 60 cm)*

LOCATION
full sun

CONDITIONS
average, well-drained soil

Salvia officinalis 'Purpurascens'

PURPLE SAGE

→ Purple sage looks terrific in the garden all year round. Left to establish itself over a few years, it will grow into a medium-sized bush. The foliage has two tones—purple and light green—which makes it especially eye-catching.

Other cultivars of *Salvia officinalis* with first-rate foliage are 'Icterina' (light green leaves with a beautiful splash of golden yellow) and 'Tricolor' (a blend of purple, pink, green and cream).

S. × *sylvestris* 'May Night' was voted Perennial Plant of the Year by the Perennial Plant Association in 1997. This compact plant has deep indigo-blue flower spikes in early summer. It grows 18 to 24 inches (45 to 60 cm) high and thrives better and lives longer in poor, sandy soil rather than fertile, humus-rich soil.

S. verticillata 'Purple Rain' produces purple flowers on short stems in July. If deadheaded, it will keep blooming for weeks, even until the frosts of October. It grows 18 inches (45 cm) high.

There are annual and biennial salvias that can deliver fabulous blue, soft pink and red flowers through summer. *S. splendens* (scarlet sage) is an attention grabber with its hot red flowers, while the mealy sage (*S. farinacea* 'Victoria') has knockout blue flowers and grows to 2 feet (60 cm) high in a sunny spot in moist but well-drained sandy soil.

JULY

Stewartia pseudocamellia

JAPANESE STEWARTIA

TYPE
tree

SIZE
*20 to 30 feet
(6 to 9 m)*

LOCATION
full sun to part shade

CONDITIONS
*moist but well-
drained soil*

JULY

➔ Stewartia is a tree with more than one season of interest. It has beautiful cup-shaped, camellia-like white flowers with showy orange-yellow stamens in July. In fall, the dark green leaves turn lovely shades of orange and burgundy-red, making it one of autumn's real head-turners.

As if all that were not enough, the tree has something extra to offer in winter. As it matures, its branches and trunk develop attractive pink, brown and grey patches.

A relatively slow-growing tree, it is the right size for a small- to medium-sized garden.

Also look for *Stewartia koreana,* which has smooth, orange-brown peeling bark and larger white flowers, and *S. monadelpha,* which has impressive orange-red-coloured bark.

Native to the woodlands of southwestern China and the hills of Nepal and India, stewartia is often listed at nurseries under the name "stuartia" because at the time of its introduction to Britain in the 18th century it was associated with John Stuart, Earl of Bute, a gifted amateur botanist.

Yucca filamentosa

ADAM'S NEEDLE

→ Yucca can act as a strong architectural feature and contribute dramatic impact and tropical style to the sunny shrub border. It not only has spectacular leaves that are sturdy and thrust upwards, it produces giant stems with dense clusters of white flowers.

Yucca is native to the southern and eastern US. 'Bright Edge' is a proven winner with striking yellow-striped leaves. Other top cultivars are 'Golden Sword', 'Color Guard', 'Variegata' and 'Ivory Tower'.

Two or three yuccas placed at intervals in a dry sunny border or rock garden can add rhythm and a change of foliage texture to the landscape. Featured as a solitary specimen in a pot or urn, the plant can have just as much impact.

Agave americana (century plant) is another superbly dramatic plant, adding a theatrical dynamic to the garden. The leaves are thick and have needle-sharp pines or edges. They can be blue-green or striped with yellow or white. It grows 30 inches to 3 feet (75 to 90 cm). Grow it in a container and move it into a frost-free spot for winter.

TYPE
shrub

SIZE
*3 to 4 feet
(90 cm to 1.2 m)*

LOCATION
full sun to part shade

CONDITIONS
sandy, well-drained soil

JULY

AUGUST

TO-DO LIST

○ *Water, water everywhere. Especially water new trees and shrubs that will be under stress and at risk from the heat; they need to be watered regularly during the first year.*

○ *Shallow-rooted rhodos and azaleas are also vulnerable to drought this month. Don't allow them to go thirsty.*

○ *Water tomatoes without getting the leaves wet to prevent fungal disease. Cover plants in exposed areas and spray with copper sulphate to prevent late-season blight.*

- ○ Make arrangements to have your pots watered if you go away on holiday. Or move them into the shade, which will slow growth and considerably reduce water loss. Especially look after valuable maples or tender potted shrubs that you treasure.
- ○ Check out ornamental grasses. See them at their peak this month.
- ○ Cool-season grass, like Calamagrostis × acutiflora 'Karl Foerster', will go dormant in the heat but will still look good and can be left right through winter.
- ○ Take pelargonium cuttings. They will easily root in 4-inch pots.
- ○ Hardy fuchsias can be easily propagated at this time by taking softwood cuttings.
- ○ Sow lettuce and radishes for fall use. Sow broccoli, spinach, green onions, kohlrabi, turnips, swiss chard, cabbage, Brussels sprouts and cauliflower for winter and spring use.
- ○ Cut back raspberry canes that produced fruit. Leave younger canes, which will be slightly green; they will bear next year's fruit.
- ○ Harvest honey figs or find a friend who grows them and beg for a taste. Mmm, so delicious.
- ○ Plant autumn-flowering crocuses (Colchicum) 4 inches (10 cm) deep, and mark the spot so you don't accidentally hoe out the flowers when they emerge.

AUGUST

Acanthus spinosus

BEAR'S BREECHES

TYPE
perennial

SIZE
*5 to 6 feet
(1.5 to 1.8 m)*

LOCATION
full sun to part shade

CONDITIONS
*moist but well-
drained soil*

➔ If you have room for it, this is a magnificent plant with handsome dark green leaves and architectural spires of two-tone (purple and white) metallic-looking flowers.

The leaves inspired the decorative detail on Corinthian columns in Roman architecture, and can also bring a classical resonance to your garden.

You do need space to accommodate it. It can grow 5 to 6 feet (1.5 to 1.8 m) high by 3 to 4 feet wide (90 cm to 1.2 m). In parts of Italy, it is still used as a ground cover under trees.

Grow it at the back of the perennial border to add dramatic structural interest. Once established, it is highly drought tolerant, although regular watering can reduce the chance of it developing mildew problems. After blooming, the plant goes dormant.

Acanthus spinosus is the most popular species. *A. mollis* is similar, almost identical, but a bigger and bolder specimen. It is used more often in larger gardens and estate gardens.

Actaea simplex 'Brunette'

BLACK BUGBANE

→ When 'Brunette' was first introduced in the 1990s, it caused a sensation. Everyone wanted it and was willing to pay a pretty penny for it. Today, it is a staple in gardens worldwide and much more reasonably priced.

It has two key attractive characteristics: beautiful, dark, purple-black foliage and fragrant, pure-white bottlebrush flowers from August into September.

The dark foliage is the perfect foil to the hot colours of canna lilies and is perfect for contrast against the golden-yellow leaves of hostas. 'Brunette' can be grown very successfully in a container too.

'Hillside Black Beauty' is so similar to 'Brunette' it is hard to tell them apart, but 'Hillside' is considered to have slightly darker foliage.

'White Pearl' is also popular with spikes of white flowers and green lacy leaves. It is shorter than 'Brunette', growing only 3 to 4 feet (90 cm to 1.2 m).

All these plants were once listed in the genus *Cimicifuga*, but taxonomists decided in 1998 that they belong in the *Actaea* family. You will still find the popular cultivars sold as cimicifuga.

TYPE
perennial

SIZE
*4 to 6 feet
(1.2 to 1.8 m)*

LOCATION
full sun to part shade

CONDITIONS
average, well-drained soil

AUGUST

Aeonium arboreum 'Schwarzkopf'

BLACK ROSE, PINWHEEL PLANT

TYPE
succulent

SIZE
*8 to 10 inches
(20 to 25 cm)*

LOCATION
full sun to light shade

CONDITIONS
sandy, well-drained soil

→ As well as having a full complement of hardy perennials, shrubs and trees, it is always important to have a few pots of frost-tender, drought-tolerant tropical plants around in summer for colour and interest.

A beautiful collector's item, aeonium is a plant to grow in a terracotta trough and to display with pride on your sunny balcony or patio all summer.

Native to the Canary Isles, it is a drought-tolerant succulent that requires minimal watering and grows into a superb foliage plant with thick, fleshy, architectural leaves in the form of rosettes.

The most popular form is a deep-purple-leaved cultivar called 'Schwarzkopf' or 'Zwartkop', but also look for *Aeonium urbicum,* which has blue-green leaves and creamy yellow flowers.

Another handsome succulent for a pot or saucer planter on your patio is echeveria, which also has thick, fleshy leaves that form an open-faced rosette. It comes in a few different colours, from soft blue to apple green with red tips.

Both aeonium and echeveria require minimum watering. In the winter, they should be brought inside where they will be perfectly happy provided they are given reasonable warmth and bright light.

Agapanthus

LILY OF THE NILE

→ The large globular blue flowers of agapanthus are definitely attractive, but if you want them in the garden you have to be a bit sneaky. Some gardeners plunge large pots of agapanthus into flower beds and fool visitors into thinking that they have been growing in that spot for years.

In reality, agapanthus is too tender to be grown outside in the majority of coastal gardens. However, in a sunny, well-protected spot, perhaps in a frost-free area close to a house or in the "California zone" of your garden, you can have success.

It helps to pick the hardiest variety. The Headbourne hybrids, a group of seedlings developed at Headbourne Worthy in Hampshire, are your best bet.

Other, arguably more attractive, cultivars include 'Back in Black', 'Midnight Blue', 'Bressingham Blue', 'Bressingham White' and 'Peter Pan'.

Native to South Africa, agapanthus dislikes boggy, heavy soil, but it also does not like ground that dries out completely, especially after the plant has flowered and is in the process of setting new flower buds. Your best bet is to grow your favourite kind in a pot and then overwinter it in a cool but frost-free greenhouse or conservatory.

TYPE
perennial

SIZE
*20 to 30 inches
(50 to 75 cm)*

LOCATION
full sun to part sun

CONDITIONS
average, well-drained soil

AUGUST

Anemone japonica ✓

JAPANESE ANEMONE

TYPE
perennial

SIZE
4 to 6 feet
(1.2 to 1.8 m)

LOCATION
part shade

CONDITIONS
average, well-drained soil

→ An essential ingredient of the late-summer garden, Japanese anemone is valued for the delicate beauty of its small white, purple or pink flowers, borne on long graceful stems. And before the flowers appear, the plant produces lush clumps of dark green, deeply cut leaves. The total package makes *Anemone japonica* a must-have performer for the August garden.

Top cultivars include 'Honorine Jobert' (white), 'Queen Charlotte', 'Whirlwind', 'Hadspen Abundance' and 'September Charm' (all pink to dark purple tones).

Although it is called "Japanese anemone," most hybrids are actually developed from one of three species that originated in China: *A. hupehensis*, *A. vitifolium* and *A. tomentosa*.

Good companions for Japanese anemones are Michaelmas daisies, such as *Aster novae-angliae* (page 221), upright stonecrops like Sedum 'Autumn Joy' (page 213) and ornamental grasses like fountain grass (*Pennisetum* 'Hameln,' page 211).

TYPE
tree

SIZE
*6 to 8 feet
(1.8 to 2.5 m)*

LOCATION
full sun

CONDITIONS
fertile, well-drained soil

Brugmansia × candida

ANGEL'S TRUMPET

→ The super-fragrant trumpet-shaped flowers of this plant can be intoxicating. Grow it in a pot on your gin-and-tonic patio and you won't know whether it's the gin or the brugmansia fragrance affecting you. It is one of the first angel's trumpets to be plucked from the mountainsides of Ecuador and shipped to Europe.

It should be stored indoors every winter, and can be pruned back if space is limited. In spring, give it a sip of 20-20-20 fertilizer, bring it back into the sunshine and watch it rise to new splendour.

It will grow quickly and by late summer will be pumping out dozens of giant, drooping, highly scented flowers. There is also a pure-white version called *Brugmansia × candida* 'Double White', which looks just as terrific.

All parts of the plant are poisonous if ingested. Treat it with respect and handle it carefully. Make sure not to rub the leaves and then wipe your eyes because the foliage contains atropine. I have grown brugmansia in a container for several years without a problem, and many other gardeners have done the same. Perhaps you will hear cautionary stories and prefer not to bother, but I still think it's a marvellous plant.

Datura meteloides also goes by the name "angel's trumpet," but cultivars of this species are short, growing only 2 to 3 feet (60 to 90 cm) high. It forms a little bush of brightly coloured flowers.

AUGUST

TYPE *shrub*

SIZE *10 to 18 inches (25 to 45 cm)*

LOCATION
full sun to part shade

CONDITIONS
average, well-drained soil

Calluna vulgaris
SUMMER-FLOWERING HEATHER

→ Most people think of heathers as winter flowering, but there are also summer-flowering heathers that can provide great colour as well as lasting foliage structure.

Most of the summer-flowering heathers are cultivars of *Calluna vulgaris*. These bloom from early summer through to fall. Some of the best were hybridized in Germany and introduced as the "garden girls."

They are called "bud bloomers" because the flowers never develop beyond the bud stage. Nevertheless, they still provide great colour for a long period. Look for 'Alexandra' (white and crimson bicolour), 'Anette' (pink), 'Sandy' (white with yellow foliage), 'Alicia' (white), 'Athene' (red), 'Amethyst' (purple) and 'Larissa' (red). Most of these will continue to provide colour into November.

More traditional summer-blooming heathers include 'Boskoop' (lavender), 'Jimmy Dyce' (lilac pink), 'County Wicklow' (shell pink), 'Firefly' (orange-red foliage and red flowers)

and 'Allegro' (dark green foliage and crimson flowers). There are dozens more.

For something a little different, there are also summer-flowering heathers in the *Erica* family. Look for the following cultivars:

- *E. × stuartii* 'Irish Lemon', 'Irish Orange' and 'Pat Turpin'
- *E. williamsii* 'David Coombe' and 'Ken Wilson'
- *E. watsonii* 'Cherry Turpin', 'Dawn' and 'Dorothy Metheny'
- *E. tetralix* 'Alba', 'George Fraser' and 'Tina'
- *E. cinerea* 'P. S. Patrick', 'Splendens' and 'Celebration'

Irish bell heather (*Daboecia*) is also very popular. The best cultivars are 'Alba' (white) and 'Arielle' (magenta).

Since they have a fibrous root system, juvenile heather plants take at least a year to get well established. They are lime haters that insist on acidic soil if they are to flourish. During the first year remember to water plants every ten days during summer.

Campis × tagliabuana 'Madame Galen'

TRUMPET VINE, TRUMPET CREEPER

→ A beautiful, hot-blooded creature, the trumpet vine has rich and deep-throated orangey red flowers that have a sensual, pouty-lipped look. This could be why hummingbirds can't stay away from it.

'Madame Galen' is a popular hybrid, resulting from crossing the Chinese trumpet creeper (*Campsis grandiflora*) and the common trumpet vine (*C. radicans*). 'Madame Galen' has salmon-red flowers and is more winter-hardy than both parents.

If it isn't soaked in sunshine, your vine will put on a lot of leafy growth and end up looking extremely lush and healthy, but it won't bloom very profusely.

Grow this vine into trees or use it to cover sheds or old tree trunks. All it needs to get started is a simple trellis or post for support. It climbs stealthily, clinging to whatever it can, using tiny aerial roots.

Prune it in early spring: trim the top to stop it from becoming too weighty, and shorten the side stems to achieve a more compact, uniform appearance.

'Indian Summer' is a cultivar that produces orange-red flowers from July to September, while *C. radicans* 'Flava' has yellow flowers.

TYPE
vine

SIZE
15 feet (4.5 m)

LOCATION
full sun

CONDITIONS
moist but well-drained soil

AUGUST

Caryopteris × clandonensis

BLUE SPIREA, BLUEBEARD

TYPE
shrub

SIZE
*30 inches to 3 feet
(75 to 90 cm)*

LOCATION
full sun

CONDITIONS
average, well-drained soil

→ Planting a spring garden is easy. It takes more foresight and planning to make sure the garden has adequate flower and foliage content in late summer. This usually involves finding spots for Japanese anemones, rudbeckia, echinacea, dahlias, ornamental grasses, Michaelmas daisies and Oriental lilies.

But caryopteris, also known as "blue spirea" or "bluebeard," is a great shrub for adding not only silvery-green or yellow foliage colour, but also powdery-blue to dark blue flowers.

To make sure you get another good show of flowers, prune it to a low framework in spring. Once established, caryopteris is fairly heat tolerant, but until then it needs to be well watered during hot spells.

Most cultivars are varieties of *Caryopteris × clandonensis*. Reliable ones include 'Dark Knight', 'Blue Mist', 'Petit Blue' and 'Longwood Blue'. 'Worcester Gold' is a gold-leaved variety, also known as "yellow-leaved spirea."

Catalpa bignonioides 'Aurea'

INDIAN BEAN TREE

→ The Indian bean tree sounds like it is from India, but it is actually native to Central America. It is loved for its bright yellow heart-shaped leaves and makes for an exotic ornamental specimen, especially when grown against the dark background of conifers.

Catalpas are called "bean trees" because in July and August the seed pods hang in bunches and resemble broad beans. The dwarf cultivar, 'Nana', is a better choice for smaller gardens, growing only 15 feet (4.5 m).

Good companions include the purple-leaved smoke bush (*Cotinus coggygria*) or *Sambucus nigra* 'Black Beauty' or 'Black Lace' (page 146), or one of the dark-purple-flowering forms of *Buddleia davidii* such as 'Black Night' or 'Dartmoor' (page 154).

Paulownia tomentosa, the empress tree, is sometimes confused with catalpa because the leaves are similar in size and shape, although the paulownia tree's leaves are coarser and hairy. The empress tree is also a bigger specimen, growing to 50 feet (15 m). It is loved for the purple foxglove-like flowers that it produces in spring.

TYPE
tree

SIZE
20 to 30 feet (6 to 9 m)

LOCATION
full sun to part sun

CONDITIONS
average, well-drained soil

AUGUST

Chasmanthium latifolium
NORTHERN SEA OATS

Clerodendrum trichotomum
HARLEQUIN GLORY BOWER

→ This short, attractive, bamboo-like grass thrives in sun or shade and produces graceful, nodding oatlike panicles that slowly turn a reddish-salmon colour in late summer.

Despite its common name, it has nothing to do with the sea. It is, however, an ideal plant for a seaside garden, being unfazed by salty air. Its graceful seed heads also look great when touched by a light sea breeze. It is native to woodlands of south-eastern North America, which is why it thrives in the shade, although it will tolerate sun.

Plant this warm-season clumping grass with other ornamental grasses such as deschampsia or carex. It also looks good mixed in with daylilies.

TYPE *ornamental grass*

SIZE *3 feet (90 cm)*

LOCATION *full sun to part shade*

CONDITIONS *moist but well-drained soil*

→ This graceful small tree from Japan is sadly undervalued and rarely seen in coastal gardens. It is deciduous, with soft, downy leaves and panicles of sweetly scented, creamy white flowers.

The flowers first appear in July and by August give way to pinkish calyxes that soften to a pale mauve-green. Purplish-blue berries in fall attract birds. The berry-laden branches can be cut and used as decorations.

It is one of the hardiest of the genus, capable of handling winter temperatures in colder areas, although it is still susceptible to prolonged sub-zero temperatures and should be planted in a reasonably sheltered spot.

Grow it as a feature tree or as a multi-stemmed shrub in the mixed border. It has a fairly broad canopy, so it is best to give it room to breathe.

TYPE *tree*

SIZE *15 to 20 feet (4.5 to 6 m)*

LOCATION *full sun to part shade*

CONDITIONS *moist but well-drained soil*

AUGUST

Coleus

SOLENOSTEMON

→ Coleus fever could be sweeping the garden world again as it once did in Britain in the last century, when wealthy gardeners were prepared to pay a small fortune to own the latest and most outrageously colourful varieties.

Coleus comes in a wide range of colours from rich burgundy and plum to deep reds or greens with purple splotches. The foliage colours are always an uplifting sight.

Four of the most striking cultivars are 'Burgundy Sun' (deep wine-red), 'Volcano' (plum-scarlet), 'Rainbow' (a mix of red, yellow, copper and pink) and 'Black Dragon' (red leaves with curled and serrated, blackish purple edges).

Even more dazzling are 'Kong Mosaic' (cherry and cream centres) and 'Rustic Red' (dark copper-orange leaves edged with green).

Cultivars in the Solar series are more sun tolerant: 'Solar Morning Mist', 'Solar Eclipse', 'Solar Flare' and 'Solar Sunrise'. All grow to 40 inches (1 m). The Sunlover series is also made for growing in full sun. Look for 'Red Ruffles', 'Rustic Orange', 'Gay's Delight' and 'Thumbelina'.

The Ducksfoot series features plants with small leaves that have the webbed look of a duck's foot. Also look for 'Indian Frills' (green leaves with a hint of purple). It is said to be more drought tolerant than other kinds.

TYPE
annual

SIZE
*12 to 18 inches
(30 to 45 cm)*

LOCATION
partial sun to light shade

CONDITIONS
*moist but well-
drained soil*

AUGUST

Cotinus coggygria 'Royal Purple'

SMOKE TREE, SMOKE BUSH

Dahlia ✓

→ The smoke bush has beautiful plum-purple, oval-shaped leaves, and gets its name from the feathery panicles of pinkish purple flowers that give the impression of puffs of smoke.

It is planted in many gardens for the pleasure of colour and contrast that its foliage provides, especially in a predominantly green shrub border or against the dark green background of a cedar or yew hedge.

Top cultivars are 'Royal Purple', 'Velvet Cloak', 'Notcutts Variety' and 'Grace'. 'Golden Spirit' has golden-yellow foliage.

Cotinus coggygria is native to southern Europe and eastward to China. It can be used as a coat-hanger plant to support summer flowering clematis such as 'Ville de Lyon' or 'Mme. Julia Correvon,' both of which have reddish flowers that perfectly complement the smoke bush's purple foliage.

TYPE *shrub*

SIZE *10 to 12 feet (3 to 3.5 m)*

LOCATION *full sun*

CONDITIONS *average, well-drained soil*

→ Something would definitely be missing if your garden had no dahlias in bloom in late summer. They offer fabulous, flamboyant flowers in a wide range of colours, shapes and sizes. The more trendy cultivars also have attractive near-black foliage.

Grown from a tuber, dahlias can be started in pots indoors in March and transplanted into the garden when the danger of frost has passed at the end of May.

Excellent are any of the cultivars in the Bishop series. They all have beautiful flowers and dark foliage. 'Bishop of Llandaff' has carmine red and is the most famous. Others include 'Bishop of Canterbury (purple), 'Bishop of Oxford' (orange), 'Bishop of York (yellow) and 'Bishop of Leicester' (lavender).

Other top dahlias with dark foliage include 'Chic' (yellow), 'Chic en Rouge' (deep red), 'Juliet' (pink), 'Romeo' (crimson), and 'Kiss' (orange).

TYPE *tuber*

SIZE *3 feet (90 cm)*

LOCATION *full sun*

CONDITIONS *average, well-drained soil*

AUGUST

Eccremocarpus scaber

CHILEAN GLORY VINE

→ If you like the challenge of growing a plant few people have in their gardens, how about giving the Chilean glory vine a whirl? It can be done. I have seen a beautiful specimen trained to drape an archway. And with a little care, you can get this tender half-hardy climber safely through winter.

It has tiny red and orange tubular flowers. Some gardeners have used it to hide the ugly bare stems of climbing roses or to cover balding spots in evergreen hedges. The Royal Horticultural Society rates it as a choice plant and has awarded it its coveted Award of Garden Merit.

The plants are not hardy but in mild regions they may survive; they die down in winter and reappear larger and stronger the following year. Plant it close to the house, and mulch to protect the roots over winter. In very mild, sheltered areas the foliage may remain all winter. Otherwise they should be treated as annuals.

One of the best cultivars is 'Tresco'.

TYPE
vine

SIZE
10 to 12 feet (3 to 3.5 m)

LOCATION
full sun

CONDITIONS
sandy, well-drained soil

AUGUST

Echinacea

PURPLE CONEFLOWER

→ Just when it looks as if the garden is running out of steam, along comes echinacea and rudbeckia and garden phlox to give it a much-needed second wind.

There have been a few significant advancements in echinacea hybridization since 2000. The first orange-blooming variety, 'Orange Meadowbrite', and its equally dynamic sister, 'Mango Meadowbrite', were developed at the Chicago Botanic Garden.

Other novelty cultivars, such as 'Razzmatazz' (rose-pink flowers with a large frilly pom-pom centre) and 'Doppelganger' a.k.a. 'Double Decker' (two layers of magenta-pink flowers), came on the market along with 'White Swan', which has white flowers with a gold and black cone at the centre.

The hottest new hybrids are members of the Big Sky series: 'Sunrise' (yellow), 'Sunset' (orange), 'Twilight' (pinkish red) and 'Sundown' (russet orange).

TYPE *perennial*

SIZE *2 to 3 feet (60 and 90 cm)*

LOCATION *full sun*

CONDITIONS *moist but well-drained soil*

Eucomis bicolor

PINEAPPLE LILY

→ Eucomis has flowers that resemble pineapples. Very cool. Grow it with chocolate cosmos, which has maroon flowers that smell like chocolate, and *Melianthus major* (page 136), which has foliage that smells like peanut butter, and you'll have a very interesting floral food garden.

This native of South Africa flowers in late summer. It is best to grow it in a pot and then tuck the pot into the flower bed. This allows you to bring the pot into a frost-free place in winter.

Bulbs have been successfully overwintered in gardens where they have been planted in sheltered, frost-free pockets, or mulched with evergreen hedge clippings to protect the bulb from frosts and excessive rain.

TYPE *bulb*

SIZE *18 inches (45 cm)*

LOCATION *full sun*

CONDITIONS *moist but well-drained soil*

AUGUST

Ficus lattarula

ITALIAN HONEY FIG

→ Imagine pulling plump, ripe fruit from a fig tree in the middle of August and eating this seductively sweet treat right on the spot with crusty French bread. This is the main reason for planting a fig tree—to get the heavenly fruit in late summer. You can also make jams and wine from it. Many Italian immigrants have perfected the art of growing figs and turned their skill into a little cottage industry.

The best kind of fig for coastal gardens is the Italian honey fig (*Ficus lattarula*). Other star cultivars, all developed from *F. carica*, include 'Peter's Honey', 'Desert King' and 'Brown Turkey'. All are hardy to Zone 7, which means they can tolerate winter temperatures of 0° to 10°F (–18 to –12°C).

They are fast-growing, but can be pruned back to a manageable height. Plant the tree in a south- or west-facing location where it will receive maximum sunshine and heat.

You need to cover it with netting in mid-July to keep starlings away and make it more difficult for raccoons to get to the fruit once it ripens, although a tree usually produces enough for everyone—humans, starlings and raccoons.

TYPE
tree

SIZE
10 feet (3 m)

LOCATION
full sun

CONDITIONS
moist but well-drained soil

AUGUST

Hakonechloa macra 'Aureola'

JAPANESE WOODLAND GRASS

Helenium

SNEEZEWEED

→ This much-admired grass has beautiful cascading bright yellow-green foliage, but what makes it even more attractive is that it thrives in the shade and brings light to dark corners. It's a good grass to grow with blue hostas.

There are two other excellent special grasses to check out:

- Japanese blood grass (*Imperata cylindrica* 'Red Baron') is a long-time favourite with rich-red foliage. It looks exceptional when backlit by the setting sun. It grows 14 to 24 inches (35 to 60 cm).

- Mexican feather grass (*Nassella tenuissima,* formerly *Stipa tenuissima)* is another winner, producing lovely clouds of feathery foliage in summer. It is extremely drought tolerant, and grows 12 to 15 inches (30 to 38 cm).

TYPE *ornamental grass*

SIZE *20 to 30 inches (50 to 75 cm)*

LOCATION *light shade*

CONDITIONS *moist but well-drained soil*

→ Sometimes called Helen's Flower, sneezeweed is one of the more attention-getting late-summer-flowering perennials. If you forgot to plant it in spring, you can buy it when you see it in bloom at the garden centre in August and find the perfect spot for it in your garden. It's good for the middle of the perennial garden.

The flower is daisy-like with a large, jewel-like cone in the centre. What makes sneezeweed so appealing, however, is the classy colour of the flowers—subtle tones of yellow, gold, orange and brown.

Top cultivars are 'Bruno' (crimson mahogany), 'Coppelia' (coppery orange), 'Butterpat' (canary yellow), 'Waltraut' (mahogany red) and 'Red and Gold' (a mix of orange, yellow and gold).

To prevent mildew problems, make sure plants get decent air circulation and are well watered during droughts.

TYPE *perennial*

SIZE *3 feet (90 cm)*

LOCATION *full sun to part shade*

CONDITIONS *moist but well-drained soil*

AUGUST

Hibiscus syriacus
ROSE OF SHARON ✓

Hosta plantaginea
AUGUST LILY, FRAGRANT HOSTA

→ Native to Syria (where it gets its species name, *syriacus*), rose of Sharon is perhaps most popular in France and Italy, where it is used extensively in parks and gardens.

It is widely admired for the beautiful blue, white or red-and-white hollyhock-like flowers it produces from August to September. After a few years it can grow into a substantial bush or it can be pruned into a small tree shape. Either way, it is a lovely sight at the end of summer.

'Blue Bird' is a star cultivar with light blue flowers with a dark centre. Other popular varieties are 'Collie Mullens' (lavender purple), 'Blushing Bride' (pink), 'Red Heart' (white with a red eye) and 'Ardens' (light purple). My personal favourites are white-flowered 'Albus' and 'White Chiffon'.

Rose of Sharon is highly disease resistant but can be slow to leaf out in cold areas. In some gardens, it has been used successfully to make a hedge.

TYPE *shrub*
SIZE *6 to 8 feet (1.8 to 2.5 m)*
LOCATION *full sun to light shade*
CONDITIONS *average, well-drained soil*

→ You will find hundreds of hostas in cultivation. Picking a select few can be a bit daunting. You start to feel as if you are overlooking some must-have specimen.

I like the hostas with blue foliage, but I have a special fondness for *Hosta plantaginea* because of its lovely pure white flowers, which have a pungent, bittersweet fragrance.

Called the August lily, the flowers are held high on sturdy stems. The pure white petals stand out at night like mini-beacons, making this hosta a good choice for a shady corner. Cultivars with yellow foliage can tolerate more sun than other kinds.

Other quality hostas to check out include 'Frances Williams', 'Great Expectations', 'June' and 'Yellow River', all of which have very striking foliage variations.

TYPE *perennial*
SIZE *2 to 3 feet (60 to 90 cm)*
LOCATION *shade or part shade*
CONDITIONS *moist but well-drained soil*

AUGUST

Hydrangea paniculata

PANICLE HYDRANGEA, PEEGEE HYDRANGEA

TYPE
shrub

SIZE
*6 to 10 feet
(1.8 to 3 m)*

LOCATION
full sun to part shade

CONDITIONS
moist but well-drained soil

→ If you have fallen in love with mophead hydrangeas (page 133) or lacecap hydrangeas (page 161), you will probably also go head over heels for the big, flouncy, cone-shape flowers of the peegee hydrangea (*Hydrangea paniculata*).

This blooms from the end of July through to September and delivers either pure white, dusty-pink or lime-green flowers. It can be clipped and trained into a small tree, sometimes as a spectacular accent plant in the centre of a lawn. The peegee hydrangea needs fertile, moisture-retentive, well-drained soil and benefits from mulching to protect the roots and to maintain moisture during the hot days of August.

This shrub is native to Japan and China. It gets it common name peegee from the "p" in *paniculata* and the "g" in 'Grandiflora', the original cultivar, which has white flowers that turn pink and was first introduced in the late 1800s.

Since then, numerous other cultivars have been hybridized including 'Burgundy Lace' and 'Pink Diamond', which have pink inflorescences, 'Kyushu', with white flowers, and 'Limelight', with lime-green flowers.

Others worth checking out are 'Praecox' and 'Unique', both of which bloom earlier in July, and 'Tardiva', which has exceptionally large panicles in August.

AUGUST

Jasminum officinale

POET'S JASMINE, COMMON WHITE JASMINE ✓ (mine blooms earlier July)

→ At its midsummer peak, the garden is so full of wonderful flower colour and fragrance, it's easy to become blasé about nature's abundance and generosity. While the great bounty of bloom might seem sufficient, it is always nice to also have the sweet scent of jasmine wafting around. It reminds you that summer is the season of plenty.

Jasminum officinale can be trained over an arch or arbour, or grown against a wall (where it requires the support of a trellis). Many gardeners use it as a backdrop near a bench where they can sit and enjoy the perfume. It can either be pruned to keep it less than 10 feet (3 m) or left to sprawl.

This jasmine is native to the Middle East and China. Being slightly tender, it won't tolerate prolonged cold spells or severe frost, so it is best to plant it in a sunny, sheltered spot in fertile, well-drained soil.

'Fiona Sunrise', also known as 'Frojas', is a top hybrid known as the hardy golden jasmine. Hybridizers have also produced 'Argenteo-variegatum', a reliable cultivar with variegated foliage.

TYPE
vine

SIZE
10 to 30 feet
(3 to 9 m)

LOCATION
full sun to part shade

CONDITIONS
moist but well-drained soil

AUGUST

Ligularia dentata 'Desdemona'

BIG LEAF LIGULARIA

→ The large, kidney-shaped purple-green leaves of 'Desdemona' make it an attractive plant right from the get-go in spring, but its value is compounded in late summer when it produces golden-yellow daisy-like flowers.

'Othello' is similar, blooming a little earlier and producing leaves that are not quite as dark.

Slugs are a notorious problem for all ligularia. Left unprotected, the leaves get chomped to shreds, even before they are fully formed. Some gardeners have success by spraying a solution of one-part ammonia and three-parts water around slug-prone plants like ligularia and hostas in early spring. If this becomes too much of a challenge or too irritating, lift the plant and grow it in a container.

Also check out the other main star of the ligularia family, *Ligularia stenocephala* 'The Rocket', which has yellow flowers spikes that soar to 4 to 6 feet (1.2 to 1.8 m) in July.

TYPE *perennial*

SIZE *3 feet (90 cm)*

LOCATION *light shade*

CONDITIONS *moist but well-drained soil*

Lilium 'Casa Blanca'

ORIENTAL LILY

→ Oriental lilies take 120 days from planting to flower. They are the grand finale in the colourful parade of Asiatic lilies that begins in June.

The white 'Casa Blanca' lily is one of best in the Oriental category. It is a fragrant show-stopper that gives the garden both class and charm.

Other outstanding varieties include 'Stargazer' (fragrant flowers with a strawberry-pink throat and creamy white edge), 'Mona Lisa' (fragrant pink flowers), 'Acapulco' (watermelon red), 'Arena' (white with red and yellow markings) and 'Montreal' (white with yellow stripes).

Grow Oriental lilies in full sun or light shade among your perennials. They will tolerate average soil but would prefer a cool root run and soil that is moist but with good drainage.

For the best effect, plant 'Casa Blanca' and other Asiatic lilies in large groups in the middle or at the back of the perennial border. Like clematis, lilies like their heads in the sun and their roots in the shade.

TYPE *bulb*

SIZE *4 feet (1.2 m)*

LOCATION *full sun to light shade*

CONDITIONS *moist but well-drained soil*

AUGUST

Lysimachia clethroides
GOOSENECK LOOSESTRIFE ✓

Molinia caerulea 'Variegata'
VARIEGATED PURPLE MOOR GRASS

→ I fell in love with this flower the moment I saw it because of its quirky gooseneck shape. In a clump, brushed by a breeze, the nodding goose heads can be mesmerizing.

Don't confuse gooseneck loosestrife with the notoriously invasive purple loosestrife (*Lythrum salicaria*). Although gooseneck loosestrife can also be an unrepentant colonizer, it can be kept within bounds by routinely slicing clumps back in size in spring or fall.

Lysimachia nummularia 'Aurea' (golden creeping jenny) is the most famous family member and has attractive golden-yellow foliage. This makes it useful as a ground cover and as an accent plant in hanging baskets or window boxes.

L. punctata, which has bright yellow flowers, is also worth getting to know. 'Alexander' is a great cultivar with variegated green and white leaves, while *L. ciliate* 'Firecracker' has burgundy-purple and yellow flowers.

TYPE *perennial*
SIZE *3 feet (90 cm)*
LOCATION *full sun to part shade*
CONDITIONS *moist but well-drained soil*

→ If you want to create a landscape completely composed of ornamental grasses, you will want to work with this special moor grass. It has beautiful creamy white-green foliage and produces airy, golden-yellow inflorescences.

Combine it with blue ornamental grasses and various heuchera for a lovely display of foliage colour. It can tolerate full sun provided it is well watered. Or grow it in the shade in dry locations. Also check out *Molinia caerulea* (purple moor grass), which grows only 12 to 16 inches (30 to 40 cm) high.

M. arundicacea 'Skyracer' is another popular cultivar. It grows 20 to 40 inches (50 cm to 1 m) high and has very graceful, erect, almost translucent foliage and classy tan-coloured inflorescences.

TYPE *ornamental grass*
SIZE *12 to 20 inches (30 to 50 cm)*
LOCATION *full sun to light shade*
CONDITIONS *moist but well-drained soil*

AUGUST

Phygelius
CAPE FUCHSIA

Rudbeckia fulgida 'Goldsturm'
BLACK-EYED SUSAN, CONEFLOWER

➜ You wouldn't know how lovely it is to have Cape fuchsias in the garden until you see a well-established clump in full bloom with lavish, teeming masses of tubular red, pink, yellow or white flowers. It can be a spectacular sight.

Native to South Africa, it is a tender perennial in most coastal gardens, which means it needs to be planted in a relatively frost-free spot, perhaps next to the south side of a wall or house, or cared for with a protective mulch in winter.

'Moonraker' and 'Yellow Trumpet' are two yellow favourites.

The Croftway series is a collection of hardier, more compact, semi-evergreen cultivars developed in Britain. Their names are 'Coral Princess', 'Purple Prince', 'Yellow Sovereign' and 'Snow Queen', which is, supposedly, the first "true white" phygelius.

Flowers in this series grow 2 to 3 feet (60 to 90 cm) and can bloom from July through to October.

TYPE *perennial*
SIZE *3 to 4 feet (90 cm to 1.2 m)*
LOCATION *full sun*
CONDITIONS *moist but well-drained soil*

➜ Rudbeckia, which is native to North America, has never been out of favour and continues to be one of the most popular perennials. It flowers at the same time as *Phlox paniculata*, *Sedum* 'Autumn Joy,' *Echinacea purpurea* and Japanese anemones (*Anemone japonica*).

'Goldsturm' is still the most garden worthy. It was named Perennial of the Year in 1999 by the Perennial Plant Association because of its disease resistance and reliability. It has also been given the Royal Horticultural Society's prestigious Award of Garden Merit.

It produces uncomplicated golden-yellow daisy-type flowers with a dark brown seed head in the centre.

Cultivars of *Rudbeckia hirta* are also widely available. These are short-lived perennials that are often treated as annuals in coastal gardens, although in the right location they can self-seed and return year after year. Top names are 'Indian Summer', 'Becky', 'Prairie Sun' and 'Irish Eyes'.

TYPE *perennial*
SIZE *2 to 3 feet (60 to 90 cm)*
LOCATION *full sun*
CONDITIONS *moist but well-drained soil*

AUGUST

Schizostylis coccinea

KAFFIR LILY, CRIMSON FLAG

→ This clump-forming perennial is native to the meadows of southern Africa. It grows from a rhizome and produces beautiful gladiolus-like spikes of pink, red or white flowers.

Each flower has six petals. They begin to appear in late August and can continue blooming until the first hard frosts of October. In mild years, they can even keep flowering into November.

Rhizomes should be planted about 12 inches (30 cm) apart. They need to be well watered since their natural habitat is beside streams.

Top cultivars are 'Mrs Hegarty' (pink), 'Sunrise' (salmon pink), 'Major' (red), 'November Cheer' (bright pink) and 'Viscountess Byng' (pale pink). 'November Cheer' and 'Viscountess Byng' are the last to flower.

TYPE *perennial*
SIZE *18 to 24 inches (45 cm to 60 cm)*
LOCATION *full sun*
CONDITIONS *average, well-drained soil*

Sorbus aucuparia

EUROPEAN MOUNTAIN ASH, ROWAN ✓

→ What a gorgeous spectacle the European mountain ash is when it is covered with countless clusters of bright orange berries.

Its common name can be confusing. European mountain ash is native to temperate parts of Europe, and its leaf is similar to that of the ash tree. But technically it doesn't belong to the ash family and is actually more closely related to the rose family, especially apples and hawthorns.

Sorbus aucuparia has white flowers in spring and produces fruit in late summer. The berries are popular with birds, especially waxwings and thrushes. As a result, the tree is spontaneously planted in gardens everywhere because the seed is distributed in bird droppings.

Top cultivars are *S. aucuparia × aronia* 'Ivan's Beauty' and *S. aucuparia × crataegus* 'Ivan's Belle', both of which have wine-red fruit.

TYPE *tree*
SIZE *20 feet (6 m)*
LOCATION *full sun*
CONDITIONS *moist but well-drained soil*

AUGUST

SEPTEMBER

→ NOTES

TO-DO LIST

○ Keep deadheading roses as well as annuals and perennials for tidiness as well as to promote continual blooming. Maintenance is the key this month.

○ Divide perennials that have become overcrowded and plant new ones that are probably being offered at bargain prices at your local garden centre.

○ Plant new peonies or lift, divide and replant established ones to create new colonies.

○ If your garden lacks pizzazz, add some late-blooming perennials such as rudbeckia, Japanese anemone, echinacea, asters and heleniums for impact.

○ Keep harvesting fruit and vegetables. Pick apples and pears and dig up and store your main crop of potatoes and carrots.

○ Collect seed from snapdragons, nicotiana and lychnis.

○ Sow seed for California and Shirley poppies as well as blue cornflowers and other hardy annuals.

○ Begin planting spring-flowering bulbs. Early planting allows them to establish a root system which enables them to get through winter more successfully.

○ Plant garlic and shallots.

○ Apply aluminum sulphate to the base of hydrangeas if you want bright blue blooms in spring. Add dolomite lime to make them pink.

○ Plant new evergreens and perennials so they will have time to develop new roots before winter.

○ Fertilize lawns with a low nitrogen, high phosphorus, potash content. Look for a 1-3-2 ratio on the bag.

SEPTEMBER

Anemanthele lessoniana

PHEASANT'S TAIL GRASS

TYPE
ornamental grass

SIZE
3 to 4 feet
(90 cm to 1.2 m)

LOCATION
full sun or light shade

CONDITIONS
average, well-drained soil

→ Some ornamental grasses have such a beautiful colour and shape they are worth growing all on their own as a feature specimen in a container. Pheasant's tail grass is one of them.

It has lovely foliage containing shades of copper, gold and bronze. The arching grass has been described as "angel's hair" for the way it waves about in a breeze. In its native New Zealand, pheasant's tail grass is also known as "gossamer grass" or "wind grass." Its beautiful colours are enhanced if it is backlit by the soft light at the end of a summer's day.

Although it can tolerate some frost, it dislikes prolonged cold periods and insists on free-draining soil. It is worth trying it in a sunny site, but it thrives best in a container where it can be moved into a sheltered location for winter.

In spring, it is usually necessary to comb out all dead foliage by running your fingers through the grass. It can self-seed, too, but if these seedlings are not wanted, they can easily be removed.

You may find it under the name *Stipa arundinacea* in some garden centres.

TYPE
perennial

SIZE
*18 to 24 inches
(45 to 60 cm)*

LOCATION
full sun to part shade

CONDITIONS
average, well-drained soil

Chrysanthemum hybrids

CUSHION MUM

→ The cushion mum has been called the "queen of autumn." These colourful high-performance hybrids turn up at garden centres in the middle of September. They are terrific for adding fall colour that can last for weeks and weeks.

Top sellers are either cultivars in the Prophet series or those that are called "Belgian mums." They are all the result of extensive years of intense hybridizing. Most of these chrysanthemums are field grown. The process is very labour intensive but the finished product is quite amazing: large, attractive dome-shaped plants with hundreds of perfectly formed flower buds that just keep blooming for weeks and weeks from September into October.

Plants usually sell for less than 15 dollars, a fantastic bargain when you consider the work that goes into producing them. Given some winter protection, they will often re-flower in May and June, giving you a second burst of blooms for your buck.

Popular varieties include 'Padre', 'Savona', 'Figari' and 'Lucera', although you are unlikely to buy a cushion chrysanthemum by its name. Instead, you are more likely to just pick out the colour you like best. Regardless, the autumn-flowering chrysanthemum is an essential ingredient of a beautiful garden in fall.

SEPTEMBER

Clematis tangutica

GOLDEN CLEMATIS

TYPE
vine

SIZE
*15 to 20 feet
(4.5 to 6 m)*

LOCATION
full sun to part sun

CONDITIONS
*average, well-
drained soil*

→ *Clematis tangutica* is a graceful, exceptionally vigorous vine that produces nodding lantern-like yellow flowers from September through to October. These are followed by equally attractive silky seed heads that often hang on into winter.

C. tangutica is useful for covering fences, pergolas or arbours or for growing against a wall. It can also be grown up into trees.

Top cultivars are 'Golden Harvest', a Dutch introduction with golden-yellow flowers that sometimes appear as early as mid-June, 'Gravetye Variety', an old favourite and 'My Angel', another Dutch hybrid with bronze-yellow flowers.

C. orientalis has similar yellow flowers but is less vigorous than *C. tangutica*. *C. paniculata* (sweet autumn clematis), which has beautiful hawthorn-scented flowers, is also worth checking out.

All of these belong to the Group-C type of clematis, which means they can be pruned to a pair of strong buds close to the ground in early spring before the new growth begins.

Colchicum

AUTUMN CROCUS

→ Colchicums are so eager to bloom you can often find the bulbs bursting into flower in their display boxes at the garden centre. They are wonderful for adding a bright splash of colour under shrubs and trees.

Plant them as soon as you get them, and they will quickly produce white, pink or purple chalice-like blooms almost immediately after hitting the ground.

The plant does not produce leaves until spring. These die away in summer and the flowers appear from September through to October. The ideal way to plant colchicum is in dense groups, 3 to 4 inches (7.5 to 10 cm) deep, 6 inches (15 cm) apart.

The name "autumn crocus" is a bit misleading as colchicum are not technically crocuses and there are crocuses that do flower in fall, such as *Crocus sativus* (the saffron crocus). Nevertheless, colchicums are still mostly referred to as autumn crocus.

They are native to Asia Minor and Europe and are poisonous. Exceptional cultivars are 'The Giant' (lilac pink with a white throat), 'Album' (brilliant white) and 'Waterlily' (large, pinkish mauve flowers with up to 20 petals).

TYPE
bulb

SIZE
*6 to 8 inches
(15 to 20 cm)*

LOCATION
full sun

CONDITIONS
*average, well-
drained soil*

SEPTEMBER

Cortaderia

PAMPAS GRASS

TYPE
ornamental grass

SIZE
*4 to 10 feet
(1.2 to 3 m)*

LOCATION
full sun

CONDITIONS
*moist but well-
drained soil*

→ The envy of gardeners who live in colder climates, pampas grass, native to South America, has showy, white, feather-duster plumes that can last all winter. Sometimes gardeners even leave them until the following summer.

Cortaderia selloana can easily grow 8 to 10 feet (2.5 to 3 m) tall by 4 feet (1.2 m) wide. Fortunately, there is *C. selloana* 'Icalma', a first-class dwarf cultivar that grows 4 to 6 feet (1.2 to 1.8 m) high and happens to be one of the hardier kinds, which means it is not damaged in cold winters.

For great impact, however, *C. richardii* is first-class with fabulous creamy plumes. *C. selloana* 'Silver Comet' is its equal with spectacular green-and-white-striped foliage.

'Sunningdale Silver' is a popular cultivar that grows to more than 10 feet (3 m) and has very dense plumes. It has been given the Award of Merit by the Royal Horticultural Society.

The leaves of cortaderia have sharp edges that can cut the skin, so don't plant it too close to a path. Maintenance is minimal: remove dead leaves and faded plumes in spring to tidy up the clump.

Eupatorium

JOE-PYE WEED

→ Joe-Pye weed is a garden giant indigenous to North America, valued for its panicles of lilac, pink or white flowers, its deep purple foliage and its sturdy upright stems that give a stately, architectural structure. Grow it as a dramatic accent plant at the back of the border.

Eupatorium purpureum subsp. *maculatum* 'Gateway' is widely popular but is also a giant of giants, growing to 10 feet (3 m) high by 8 feet (2.5 m) wide.

'Flore Pleno' is more manageable for medium-sized gardens. 'Little Joe' is even more compact, growing to only 4 feet (1.2 m).

Some experts regard *E. coelestinum*, which has light blue ageratum-like flowers, the prettiest of the bunch. 'Chocolate' has purple-brown leaves and white flowers and looks very good underscored with the yellow flowers of coreopsis.

TYPE *perennial*
SIZE *4 to 10 feet (1.2 to 3 m)*
LOCATION *full sun to part shade*
CONDITIONS *moist but well-drained soil*

Miscanthus sinensis

JAPANESE SILVER GRASS

→ Unlike cool-season grasses that are virtually evergreen in coastal gardens, miscanthus requires warm soil before it can really get going. It looks pretty awful when you buy it in spring, but will transform into something awesome by late summer. By September it can be quite big, bold and spectacular.

'Gold Bar' is an exciting cultivar with golden-yellow horizontal stripes and burgundy inflorescences. Experts rate it as a much better plant than its cousins, 'Strictus' (porcupine grass) and 'Zebrinus' (zebra grass).

'Morning Light' is another top performer with handsome green and white variegated foliage that has a pinkish hue. 'Gracillimus' (maiden grass) offers impact and is also well-behaved and easy to accommodate.

Dwarf cultivars like 'Yaku Jima', 'Adagio' and 'Little Kitten', all of which grow to 3 to 4 feet (90 cm to 1.2 m), are better picks for small- to medium-sized gardens.

TYPE *ornamental grass*
SIZE *4 to 5 feet (1.2 to 1.5 m)*
LOCATION *full sun to light shade*
CONDITIONS *average, well-drained soil*

SEPTEMBER

Passiflora caerulea

BLUE PASSION VINE

TYPE
vine

SIZE
*15 to 20 feet
(4.5 to 6 m)*

LOCATION
full sun

CONDITIONS
*average, well-
drained soil*

→ Everyone who sees the extraordinary flowers of the blue passion vine for the first time can't help but fall under its spell. Most people are immediately enchanted by the amazing intricacy and uniqueness of the flower.

Each flower has ten petals, which provide a decorative backdrop for a skirt, or fringe, of purplish blue bristles. Above the bristles, there are five green stamens with three more purple-coloured stamens above them. The whole complex construction is superb.

The vine also has attractive glossy green foliage, which in mild areas stays green all winter. At the end of summer, flowers give way to yellow passion fruit. These are edible but have very little flavour.

Passiflora caerulea, native to Brazil and Argentina, is the most viable species for coastal gardens. It is vigorous and can easily cover a large wall 15 by 20 feet (4.5 by 6 m). Plant it against a south- or west-facing wall in a relatively frost-free location.

'Constance Elliott' is a scented, white-flowering cultivar that is said to be hardier than the blue kind. It was given a first-class certificate by the British Royal Horticultural Society in 1884 and has been observed to survive in mild areas provided it is protected from heavy frost.

SEPTEMBER

Pennisetum alopecuroides

FOUNTAIN GRASS

→ Fountain grass is suitable for planting in dense drifts and mixing with perennials like rudbeckia, echinacea, upright sedum, asters and Japanese anemone.

Pennisetum alopecuroides is a good pick for a drought-tolerant, water-wise landscape. It produces a lovely show of white or tan bottlebrush spikes. Top cultivars are 'Hameln', 'Little Bunny' and 'Moudry', which has almost black inflorescence.

P. orientale (Oriental fountain grass) is similar. Reliable cultivars are 'Tall Tails' and 'Karley Rose', which has dusty-rose inflorescence.

P. setaceum 'Rubrum' (purple-leaved fountain grass) is one of the bestselling grasses because of its adorable, pinkish purple foxtail plumes that cascade on arching stems above a clump of lush purple foliage. It grows about 18 inches (45 cm) high.

P. messiacum is also a species worth knowing, especially a cultivar like 'Red Bunny Tails', which has burgundy, cattail-like flowers.

TYPE
ornamental grass

SIZE
2 to 3 feet
(60 to 90 cm)

LOCATION
full sun

CONDITIONS
moist but well-drained soil

SEPTEMBER

Rhus typhina 'Tiger Eyes'

STAGHORN SUMAC

TYPE
tree

SIZE
6 to 8 feet
(1.8 to 2.5 m)

LOCATION
sun to part shade

CONDITIONS
average, well-drained soil

→ Most people notice the staghorn sumac for the first time in autumn when its leaves turn bright red and shades of orange. But this tree, native to eastern North America, is also regarded as a very useful foliage shrub for a container or planter box, or as part of a drought-tolerant planting scheme in a water-saving garden.

'Tiger Eyes' is a handsome cutleaf sumac that was introduced in 2004 by a Minnesota nursery. Great in the garden or in a container, 'Tiger Eyes' has attractive chartreuse leaves that turn bright yellow in late summer.

By autumn, the leaves change colour again, turning a mixture of orange, yellow and scarlet. Unlike the common species, which grows to 15 feet (4.5 m), 'Tiger Eyes' makes an ideal tree or shrub for small gardens as well as for growing in a container on a balcony or patio.

SEPTEMBER

TYPE
perennial

SIZE
*18 to 24 inches
(45 to 60 cm)*

LOCATION
full sun

CONDITIONS
average, well-drained soil

Sedum × 'Autumn Joy'

SHOWY STONECROP

→ Every coastal garden has this plant somewhere. Its fabulous sculptural elegance, great flower colour and total reliability make it too valuable to leave out. Although other cultivars have risen to challenge it, 'Autumn Joy' remains at the top of the list.

It gives excellent value for money from the moment it resurfaces in spring to the time its sturdy pink flower heads add warmth, character and charm to the garden in late summer. And the stems and flower heads are sturdy enough that they can be left over the winter to provide colour and structure.

This disease-, drought- and pest-resistant plant has thick, fleshy, succulent leaves. It is best grown in dense drifts, but it can also be featured in a container or as a single addition at the front of the herbaceous border.

Other top cultivars are 'Matrona', which has grey-green foliage with plum-red stems and large, soft pink flower heads; 'Black Jack', which is very similar to 'Matrona', with solid dark purple foliage; and 'Brilliant', which is more compact and a brighter pink than 'Autumn Joy'.

'Autumn Fire' is another updated version of 'Autumn Joy' with flowers that are said to last longer. 'Blade Runner' is a novelty hybrid with reddish purple flowers, while 'Cloud Walker' has pinkish purple flowers and dark foliage.

SEPTEMBER

Tricyrtis
TOAD LILY

TYPE
perennial

SIZE
2 feet (60 cm)

LOCATION
shade

CONDITIONS
*moist but well-
drained soil*

SEPTEMBER

→ Unlike any other flower in the garden, the toad lily has orchid-like blooms peppered with purple spots and blotches. The plant is fast becoming one of the must-haves in the gardening world, and gardeners are starting to pride themselves on having collections.

Native to Japan, this woodland perennial is sometimes referred to as the "Jewel of the Orient" and makes an excellent companion for hardy ferns, hostas, hellebores and erythroniums (page 105). They bloom from the end of summer into autumn and thrive in light shade where the soil is rich in organic matter that never dries out completely.

Most popular cultivars are forms of either *Tricyrtis hirta* or *T. formosana*, although there are at least 55 species and cultivars in current cultivation.

Names to ask for include 'Hatatogisa' (purple), 'Shirohotogisu' (white), 'Tojen' (lavender purple), 'Miyazaki' (pink with crimson spots) and 'Miyazaki Gold' (similar to 'Miyazaki', but has leaves edged with creamy gold). Newer introductions include 'Raspberry Mousse', 'Empress' and 'Dark Beauty'.

Verbena bonariensis

BRAZILIAN VERBENA

→ I first saw the lovely tall purple flowers of *Verbena bonariensis* in Cornwall, England, where they were planted en masse at the Lost Gardens of Heligan. I was instantly impressed by its fabulous colour and the slender but sturdy and erect stems, which hold up tight clusters of purple flowers.

On investigation, I discovered it was actually native to Brazil and Argentina. I also found out that it grows everywhere in the southeastern US as well as Texas and all over California. Apparently, it started out in gardens, then escaped into the wild.

This short-lived perennial can become invasive as it seeds profusely. Try to control its seed production within the first couple of years, although with the wetness of our winters, the rate of germination is often considerably reduced.

Gardeners who live in competition with deer and rabbits will be pleased to know that *V. bonariensis* is said to be resistant to both these critters. It is also a good pick for a drought-tolerant planting scheme. The Royal Horticultural Society has honoured it with an Award of Garden Merit.

TYPE
perennial

SIZE
3 to 4 feet (90 cm to 1.2 m)

LOCATION
full sun

CONDITIONS
average, well-drained soil

SEPTEMBER

OCTOBER

→ NOTES

TO-DO LIST

○ Move tender plants like pelargoniums, brugmansia, fuchsia, phormium and tibouchina back into the greenhouse or a frost-free place for winter.

○ Lift dahlias, wash off tubers and store them in a frost-free place for winter.

○ Empty flower beds of annuals once they have been exposed to frost.

○ Wrap the pseudo-trunk of your hardy banana tree with bubble wrap to preserve it over winter.

○ Plant spring-flowering bulbs. Start by bulking up the garden with mostly naturalizing bulbs such as species tulips, snowdrops, crocuses, muscari and scillas before planting basic tulips and narcissi.

○ Plant new trees and shrubs and move shrubs to a better location.

○ Fill containers with a triple-decker planting of bulbs to create a sequence of blooms in spring. Store out of the rain.

○ Plant wallflowers in sunny, sheltered places where they will provide ground cover over winter and flowers in April and May. Gardeners in Victoria do this very well.

○ Get yours hedges trimmed by a professional to ensure they have a sleek, clipped, sculpted look.

○ Harvest the last of the tender vegetables (such as zucchini and squash) before frost. Brussels sprouts, carrots, cabbage and turnips can be left until later.

OCTOBER

Acer japonicum 'Aconitifolium'

FERN-LEAF MAPLE

TYPE
tree

SIZE
*15 to 20 feet
(4.5 to 6 m)*

LOCATION
part sun to light shade

CONDITIONS
*average, well-
drained soil*

→ The late J. D. Vertrees, an expert on the American maple, described 'Aconitifolium' as "never weak or willowy" and as having "brilliant scarlet tones." That's a very solid endorsement for a tree. I have planted it in two places in my own garden to flank steps. In October, when the nights get cooler, the leaves of 'Aconitifolium' do indeed turn a spectacular scarlet colour.

Fall is a good time to plant this tree, or any tree for that matter. In my opinion, fall planting is better than spring planting because it allows the tree to establish its roots. In spring, a tree has very little time to get established before it comes under the stress of hot days.

All Japanese maples can take full sun but are happier and look better in dappled shade. They respond well to pruning but generally do not need it, especially when planted with enough room to grow.

Aconitum × carmichaelii 'Arendsii'

AZURE MONKSHOOD, AUTUMN MONKSHOOD

→ With beautiful tall spires of hooded bright blue flowers, 'Arendsii' is a good plant for putting colour into the back of the herbaceous border.

It thrives in the woodland garden and has a sturdy stem with deep green foliage. It is a good companion for ornamental grasses and Japanese anemones.

Over the centuries, it has earned a rather exaggerated reputation as a killer plant because it has poison in its sap. But it can be handled safely and is even becoming rather popular with florists in Europe who use it as a cut flower.

However, it is sensible to always wash your hands after working with aconitum, and to keep children and pets away from it.

Other cultivars that flower in midsummer include *Aconitum napellus* 'Carneum', with soft-pink flowers, and *A. × cammarum* 'Bicolor', which has white flowers with a blue edge. 'Bressingham Spires' is a more compact hybrid that does not require staking. It has deep violet-blue flowers in July.

TYPE
perennial

SIZE
*4 to 6 feet
(1.2 to 1.8 m)*

LOCATION
full sun to part shade

CONDITIONS
moist but well-drained soil

OCTOBER

Aronia melanocarpa 'Autumn Magic'

BLACK CHOKEBERRY

TYPE
shrub

SIZE
4 to 6 feet
(1.2 to 1.8 m)

LOCATION
full sun to part shade

CONDITIONS
average, well-drained soil

➔ 'Autumn Magic' usually catches the eye when it is covered in elegant black berries that stand out in beautiful contrast to the shrub's light green foliage.

When buying a plant, gardeners should always ask, "Does this give me more than one season of interest?" Flowers are nice, but a plant ought to have other winning characteristics to make it garden-worthy. 'Autumn Magic', a cultivar that was developed at the University of BC Botanical Garden, does have these other qualities.

In spring, it produces small, creamy white flowers, beautifully set against waxy, light green foliage. But its main appeal is that from late summer into autumn it covers itself with clusters of shiny purple-black berries. (They attract birds and are a favourite snack of robins.) And when the days turn cooler in late fall, the foliage turns bright red.

Aronia likes to colonize its space, so you need to keep an eye out for suckers, which can easily be removed. To propagate a plant for a friend, take softwood cuttings in late spring or early summer.

TYPE
perennial

SIZE
2 to 4 feet
(60 cm to 1.2 m)

LOCATION
full sun to part shade

CONDITIONS
average, well-drained soil

Aster

MICHAELMAS DAISY

→ One of the last perennials to flower in the year, asters provide a spectacular show of colour from the end of September into October.

They bloom around the feast of St. Michael, which is September 29, and that's how they get their name. They range in size from gangly 5-foot (1.5 m) giants to compact dwarf specimens that can be easily accommodated in a rockery.

The best kinds for the average garden are cultivars of *Aster × frikartii*. They bloom for a long time, starting in midsummer and on into fall.

Star performers are 'Monch', which has bright, lavender-blue flowers with yellow centres, 'Flora's Delight', with lilac-mauve flowers and a yellow eye, and 'Wunder von Stafa' (a.k.a. 'Wonder of Stafa'), with light blue flowers.

These all grow 18 to 30 inches (45 and 75 cm) high in full sun and fertile soil that stays moist in summer. 'Monch' is very resistant to powdery mildew, is exceptionally free-flowering and produces a lot of flowers from July to October.

A. novi-belgii (New York aster) is taller, growing to 3 to 4 feet (90 cm to 1.2 m). Top cultivars are 'Coombe Rosemary' (violet-purple), 'Royal Ruby' (deep red), 'Coombe Margaret' (reddish pink), 'Ada Ballard' (mauve-blue) and 'Patricia Ballard' (pink).

A. novae-angliae (New England aster) grows to 5 feet (1.5 m) high and benefits from being pinch-pruned at the tips in early July, which makes it bushier. Top names include 'Purple Dome', 'September Ruby', 'Mrs. S. T. Wright' and 'Harrington's Pink'.

OCTOBER

Aucuba japonica

SPOTTED LAUREL

TYPE
shrub

SIZE
6 feet (1.8 m)

LOCATION
full sun or part shade

CONDITIONS
moist but well-drained soil

→ Evergreen shrubs with variegated foliage are useful for adding interest to the garden in winter as well as structure year round.

Aucuba is an old favourite that thrives in both full sun and part shade, although it is invariably planted in shady spots because the foliage brightens dark corners. It is valued for its evergreen leaves, which are splattered with yellow blotches.

Aucuba can be mass-planted and clipped to make a formal hedge, planted along with rhododendrons, camellias and azaleas in the shrub border or can even be featured as a solitary stand-alone specimen in a container.

Top cultivars are 'Crotonifolia', 'Picturata', 'Nana' (dwarf form), 'Golden King' and 'Gold Dust'. Since plants are both female and male it's necessary to have both a female and male plant in close proximity if you want berries. However, most gardeners are satisfied with the foliage colour and may be less interested in ensuring that the plant produces berries.

Aucuba enjoyed considerable popularity during Victorian times. It was widely planted in parks and other public places around Britain, but then it quickly fell out of favour. The Dutch are now starting to revive that interest by producing new varieties that are sold as houseplants.

Callicarpa bodinieri var. *giraldii* 'Profusion'

BEAUTYBERRY

Carex morrowii 'Ice Dance'

SEDGE

→ 'Profusion' produces beautiful clusters of shiny lavender-purple berries that are just as pretty as flowers, and which linger on bare branches for a month or longer.

Callicarpa is best planted in a spot where the berries can be easily seen and enjoyed. It looks exceptionally good set against a white wall, but also looks natural in a woodland setting.

If it is grown against a wall or fence, all you need to do is prune the shrub regularly for size in order to create a sturdy, semi-formal framework.

I always recommend this deciduous shrub when people ask what to plant to give colour and interest to the garden in fall and winter.

In spring, the shrub's juvenile foliage is purplish bronze. This can be cut and brought indoors for use as a table decoration as can the bare branches loaded with purple berries in fall.

TYPE *shrub*

SIZE *6 feet (1.8 m)*

LOCATION *full sun to part shade*

CONDITIONS *average, well-drained soil*

→ The sedge family has some outstanding grasses. 'Ice Dance' is one of the best with strong green-and-white-striped arching leaves that stay attractive all year round.

Use it in the garden to fill gaps at the front of the perennial border or make a display of it in a container.

'Evergold' is similar but does not perform quite as well as 'Ice Dance' over a long period.

Other top carex grasses:

- *Carex elata* 'Aurea' (a.k.a. 'Bowles Golden') is a beautiful golden-yellow grass.
- *C. flagellifera* and *C. buchananii* both have lovely bronze foliage.
- 'Frosted Curls' has fine green leaves that look like a wild, moplike head of uncombed hair.
- *C. testacea* is one of my favourites because of its striking coppery-orange foliage.

TYPE *ornamental grass*

SIZE *8 to 12 inches (20 to 30 cm)*

LOCATION *part shade*

CONDITIONS *average, well-drained soil*

OCTOBER

Cotoneaster dammeri

BEARBERRY COTONEASTER

TYPE
shrub

SIZE
*6 to 8 inches
(15 to 20 cm)*

LOCATION
full sun to part shade

CONDITIONS
average, well-drained soil

→ Cotoneaster is a great choice if you are trying to achieve a low-maintenance garden. It is tough and disease resistant and doesn't mind being pruned back hard.

Its attractive glossy evergreen leaves make it a first-rate ground cover, and its tiny white flowers in spring and red berries in fall provide the added bonus of visual interest.

Cotoneaster dammeri is a good pick to grow over banks because of its perfect prostrate nature, or you can train it to tumble over a low retaining wall. Top cultivars are 'Eichholz', 'Coral Beauty' and 'Lowfast'. They all have bright, orange-red berries in fall.

Also check out *Gaultheria procumbens* (wintergreen), which is often used to dress up winter containers. It is an excellent low-growing ground cover with glossy deep green leaves and red berries in winter. The best cultivar is 'Macrocarpa', which grows to 6 inches (15 cm) high by 3 feet (90 cm) wide.

TYPE
perennial

SIZE
*9 to 12 inches
(23 to 30 cm)*

LOCATION
full sun to part shade

CONDITIONS
average, well-drained soil

Heuchera hybrids

CORAL BELLS

→ Today, coral bells are one of the world's bestselling perennials. This wasn't always the case. Heuchera's astonishing transformation from ugly duckling to star performer is one of horticulture's most fascinating success stories.

It comes down to some amazingly creative hybridizing in the 1990s, especially by horticulturists like Dan Heims of Terra Nova Nurseries in Portland, Oregon. Nine of his hybrids have won the Award of Garden Merit by the Royal Horticultural Society.

Why do experienced gardeners love coral bells so much? Because we know that the fabulous colour or texture of foliage can have just as much impact and lasting value as any flower.

'Plum Pudding' is one of the best. It has plum-coloured leaves that have

a metallic, pewter-grey finish. Other top hybrids are 'Purple Petticoats', 'Chocolate Ruffles', 'Stormy Seas', 'Can Can', 'Pewter Veil' and 'Amber Waves', which has since been outperformed by its big brother, 'Marmalade'.

Most of these hybrids dislike too much exposure to direct afternoon sun, so plant them where they get light shade in the afternoon. The airy sprays of white, red or pink flowers can be cut and used in flower arrangements.

Since they hold their foliage through the winter, these are great plants for winter containers, along with ajuga and cool-season ornamental grasses.

OCTOBER

Nerine bowdenii
CAPE FLOWER

→ How do we know winter is coming early? The nerines bloom early. At least, some gardeners believe that this is a sure sign of an early winter.

Native to South Africa, most kinds of nerine are too tender to be grown in coastal gardens, but *Nerine bowdenii* is a hardy species and able to tolerate our winters, provided bulbs are planted in a well-drained site. Plant them in spring in a sunny location, perhaps against a south-facing wall.

N. bowdenii produces bright pink flowers from the end of September through October on bare stems. The leaves don't appear until spring. Clumps can be left to bulk up for a few years before being divided and used to form new colonies. Top pink cultivars are 'Mark Fenwick' and 'Pink Triumph'. There is also a white cultivar simply called 'Alba'.

TYPE *bulb*

SIZE *18 inches (45 cm)*

LOCATION *full sun*

CONDITIONS *average, well-drained soil*

Sciadopitys verticillata
JAPANESE UMBRELLA PINE

→ Why this attractive conifer is not grown more widely in coastal gardens is a mystery. The dense whorls of glossy green needles resemble the spokes of an umbrella. They are long, soft and pleasant to touch. The tree also has an attractive orangey red bark.

Feed this tree, which is hardy to Zone 6, plenty of nitrogen, and the foliage will stay a lustrous green rather than turning anemic yellow.

The umbrella pine is native to Japan. As with the ginkgo tree (*Ginkgo biloba*) and Wollemi pine (*Wollemia nobilis*), there is fossil evidence that this dates back two hundred million years to the days of the dinosaur.

TYPE *tree*

SIZE *15 to 20 feet (4.5 to 6 m)*

LOCATION *full sun to light shade*

CONDITIONS *moist but well-drained soil*

OCTOBER

Viola cornuta hybrids

WINTER PANSY

→ Brighten up your garden in October by filling containers, troughs and window boxes with cultivars of *Viola cornuta*, which are better known as winter pansies.

This common name is a little misleading. While winter pansies certainly add colour to the garden in autumn, they tend to go dormant in most coastal gardens during the coldest months of winter.

At times they may appear to have wilted and died, but surprisingly they do bounce back with great vigour in spring and can flower beautifully from April to June.

These come in a wide assortment of colours, mostly beautiful two-tone shades of blue, yellow and maroon. Use them to add a generous splashes of colour to your front entrance from late September to November and to provide a striking flush of flowers in spring.

TYPE
perennial

SIZE
6 to 10 inches (15 to 25 cm)

LOCATION
part sun

CONDITIONS
average, well-drained soil

OCTOBER

NOVEMBER

TO-DO LIST

○ *Prune back summer-flowering clematis (C-types such as* Clematis jackmanii*) and pull away the dead mass of stems. Don't prune clematis that flower on old wood. Do this after they have bloomed.*

○ *Deadhead roses for the last time this season and prune lightly for winter. Cut back rose bushes by a third to prevent them being rocked and their roots dislodged by wind.*

- ○ Finish planting spring-flowering bulbs—tulips, daffodils, crocuses and snowdrops—and don't miss the chance to fill the garden with several varieties of allium, especially Allium aflatunense and A. christophii.
- ○ Plant new hedges and move conifers that have been growing in containers into permanent locations in the garden.
- ○ Prepare the ground where you intend to plant bare-root roses over winter.
- ○ Plant a container for winter colour: try heuchera, skimmia, euphorbia, gaultheria, nandina and ajuga as well as variegated shrubs like euonymous, pieris and aucuba and grasses like Carex 'Evergold'.
- ○ Rake leaves. Use disease-free leaves around shrubs as a natural mulch, and shred the rest with your lawn mower and add to the compost bin.
- ○ Do not cut every grass and perennial to the ground in your cleanup. Many of them can look very attractive left to be beautified by frosts and snow over winter.
- ○ Apply dolomite lime to lawns to reduce acidity caused by winter rains. Liming "sweetens" the soil by raising the pH (the measure of the acidity or alkalinity—the higher the pH, the more alkaline). Grass requires a medium pH, neither too acidic or too alkaline.
- ○ Start amaryllis bulbs indoors. Early varieties will bloom in time for Christmas.

NOVEMBER

TYPE
shrub

SIZE
*6 to 8 feet
(1.8 to 2.5 m)*

LOCATION
part sun to light shade

CONDITIONS
average, well-drained soil

Camellia sasanqua

→ Can you believe that flowers this beautiful bloom in winter?

Britain's climate is not that different from ours, and the Royal Horticultural Society reported that on January 1, 2007, at least 11 cultivars of *Camellia sasanqua* were in bloom at its famous Wisley garden in Surrey. We should be encouraged by this and plant more of these unusual and spectacular early-blooming camellias. Placed in the right spot, they can give us wonderful colour from November to January.

C. sasanqua is the earliest flowering camellia, but it has good and bad years. If it rains too much, the flowers can be spoiled. But in drier years, the flowers can be spectacular.

One of the best sasanquas is 'Bonanza', which has red flowers in fall. Other top cultivars include 'Yuletide', 'Sparkling Burgundy', 'Kanjiro', 'Jean May', 'Autumn Moon', 'Narumigata', 'Autumn Sunrise' and 'Winter's Snowman'.

C. sasanqua is native to the evergreen coastal forests of southern Japan, and has attractive glossy foliage. Camellias provide year-round structure as well as good screening. You can tell a cultivar of *C. sasanqua* from its more common, spring-flowering cousin, *C. japonica* (page 44), by the fuzziness of the stems and the smaller, more refined shape of the leaf.

They all prefer an east-facing location, ideally in a woodland setting with rhododendrons and azaleas.

Cyclamen hederifolium

HARDY CYCLAMEN

→ With dainty pink flowers that resemble tiny butterfly wings, *Cyclamen hederifolium* also produces a carpet of beautifully ivy-shaped, marbled leaves that can stay attractive for nine months of the year. There is a white variety, 'Alba', that some find more attractive than the one with pink flowers.

It is especially attractive when grown under shrubs and around trees in the woodland garden and can also be planted in shady parts of the rock garden. As tough as old boots, its flowers first appear before the leaves, but the leaves themselves can give interest for a long time before the plant goes dormant for a brief period of time in summer.

It has no serious pest or disease problems, and although it gets its species name, *hederifolium*, from its resemblance to ivy, it is far more delicate looking and less invasive than ivy. Squirrels sometimes dig up the corms, which are prone to rot if planted in poorly drained soil.

TYPE
perennial

SIZE
*4 to 6 inches
(10 to 15 cm)*

LOCATION
part shade

CONDITIONS
*humus-rich, moist but
well-drained soil*

NOVEMBER

TYPE *shrub*

SIZE *8 to 14 inches (20 to 35 cm)*

LOCATION
full sun

CONDITIONS
average, well-drained soil

Erica carnea/Erica darleyensis

WINTER-FLOWERING HEATHER

→ A little bit of erica in your life can brighten up the winter garden to no end. We all call it "heather"—even if technically it is a "heath."

Most cultivars have green foliage, but some can have golden-yellow or orange-yellow foliage. With the right selection, you can have flowers or bright foliage interest from early winter through to spring.

November is a good month to check out all the various ericas, pick out the ones you like and then plant them where they will be most appreciated. Do this as long as the ground is not frozen solid or sodden from heavy rains.

'Darley Dale' (shell pink), 'George Rendall' (purple) and 'Ghost Hills' (pink) are all cultivars of *Erica darleyensis* that are capable of blooming very early in November. Other top hybrids in this category include 'Kramer's Red' (magenta flowers and bronze-green foliage), 'White Perfection' (brilliant white flowers and light green foliage), 'Silberschmelze' (silver white flowers), 'Darley Dale' (pale mauve flowers) and 'Mary Helen' (pink flowers and golden-yellow foliage).

E. carnea is another very popular species that flowers in winter. First cultivars to bloom are 'Schneekuppe' (white), 'Myretoun Ruby' (ruby red), 'December Red' (pink) and 'Springwood' (white). There are at least 125 other named cultivars, according to the Scottish Heather Society.

Avoid putting them in ground that is either too damp or too dry. Heavy, clay-based soil is a killer. Prepare the planting site by adding well-rotted compost.

Prune your winter heathers when they have finished flowering—if you don't they can look messy. As well, heathers always look better when you combine a few different types to achieve a tapestry of colour year round. To make this happen, you'll need to include summer-flowering heathers like *Calluna vulgaris* (page 184).

NOVEMBER

Ginkgo biloba

MAIDENHAIR TREE

→ One of the world's oldest trees, there is fossil evidence that the ginkgo was around at the time of the dinosaurs. It remains a superb specimen, and is an ideal city-street tree since it is highly disease resistant and tolerant of air pollution.

What endears this tree to many gardeners is its distinctive fan-shaped leaves that turn bright yellow in the fall, transforming the canopy into what can look like thousands of fluttering butterflies.

Two top cultivars are 'Autumn Gold', which has excellent golden-yellow fall colour and a pyramidal shape, and 'Princeton Sentry', which has a slightly more vertical shape, like an architectural column. 'Autumn Gold' is regarded as the superior of the two. ('Tubifolia' is a more unusual cultivar with rolled leaves.)

They both grow 10 to 15 feet (3 to 4.5 m) high in the first ten years and then develop more slowly thereafter. They can reach heights of 40 to 50 feet (12 to 15 m) at maturity.

TYPE
tree

SIZE
*40 to 50 feet
(12 to 15 m)*

LOCATION
full sun

CONDITIONS
average, well-drained soil

NOVEMBER

TYPE
shrub

SIZE
8 feet (2.5 m)

LOCATION
full sun to light shade

CONDITIONS
moist but well-drained soil

Ilex × meserveae

MESERVE HYBRID HOLLY

→ Although the red berries of the holly bush are an enduring Christmas symbol, they are a cheerful winter sight in general, especially against the white background of a fresh snowfall.

The most popular cultivars are hybrids of English holly (*Ilex aquifolium*), which produces striking blood-red berries and glossy deep-green leaves. However, English holly (which is native to Britain and not North America) has become regarded as an invasive species. Gardeners are no longer encouraged to plant it. Instead, they are pointed to "safe" cultivars that produce attractive berries but sterile seed that won't germinate and so can never become invasive.

Best of these risk-free hollies are cultivars of *I. × meserveae,* such as 'Blue Girl', 'Blue Boy', 'China Boy', 'China Girl', 'Blue Maid', 'Blue Prince' and 'Blue Princess'. To get berries, you need a male and female plant. You can tell the sex of any holly in most cases by the gender of the name. There are exceptions, however. 'Silver Queen', for instance, sounds like it should be a female, berry-bearing type, but it is actually a male cultivar, while *I. altaclerensis* 'Golden King' is female.

A few hollies are self-fertile, which means they are capable of producing berries without a pollinating partner. A long-time favourite is *I. aquifolium* 'J. C. van Tol', which grows to 15 feet (4.5 m) and has bright red berries and leaves that are less prickly than other hollies.

A quirky holly worth knowing is the hedgehog or porcupine holly (*I. aquifolium* 'Ferox Argentea'). Although it does produce fertile seed, it is considered far less invasive than other *I. aquifolium* cultivars because it is very compact and slow-growing.

Nandina domestica

HEAVENLY BAMBOO, SACRED BAMBOO

→ An outstanding plant all year round, heavenly bamboo is especially useful for providing foliage interest as well as a colour and architectural accent in the winter. It can add refinement to an entranceway or disguise the ugly stems of a climbing rose.

As well as having exquisite foliage, which ranges from reddish purple to lime-green with red to crimson highlights, nandina produces dainty clusters of tiny flower buds followed by red berries.

Native to China and Japan, where it grows in the dappled shade of woodlands, it gets its common name "heavenly bamboo" partly from being planted around temples and shrines in Asia, and partly from its resemblance to bamboo. It is actually not related to bamboo at all, but is rather a member of the barberry family.

The common species, *Nandina domestica*, has yellow-green foliage. 'Plum Passion' is a cultivar with striking purple foliage.

Dwarf cultivars, such as 'Gulf Stream' and 'Harbor Dwarf', grow to 3 feet (90 cm). Also look for 'Wood's Dwarf', 'Moon Bay' and 'Nana' (a.k.a. 'Pygmaea'). They all have attractive young leaves with a pink or reddish tinge in spring.

For something a little different, try *N. domestica* var. *leucocarpa*, which has bright, light-green foliage and white berries, and 'Firepower', which grows only 2 feet (60 cm) high and has lime-green leaves.

TYPE
shrub

SIZE
*6 to 8 feet
(1.8 to 2.5 m)*

LOCATION
sun to part shade

CONDITIONS
average, well-drained soil

NOVEMBER

Pyracantha 'Orange Glow'

FIRETHORN

TYPE
shrub

SIZE
6 to 8 feet
(1.8 to 2.5 m)

LOCATION
full sun to part shade

CONDITIONS
average, well-drained soil

→ This is one of the most useful winter berry-bearing shrubs for providing long-lasting colour as well as structural interest. It is also a very hardy, disease-resistant plant, capable of thriving in a wide range of challenging situations, including shaded and full-sun sites.

A member of the rose family, pyracantha is native to southeastern Europe and central China. Its orange, yellow or red berries, which appear in abundant clusters from the end of November, are a favourite of blackbirds.

Most popular cultivars are a form of *Pyracantha coccinea*: 'Orange Glow', 'Mohave', 'Lalandei' and 'Golden Charmer' are all excellent picks.

Try to get any pruning done in late winter or early spring. But some gardeners prefer to wait until they see flowers—pruning carefully so as not to remove too many flowers since they produce the berries in fall. (Both flowers and berries are only produced on old growth.) Pyracantha can then be lightly pruned a couple of times throughout the summer to keep it sculpturally shaped against a fence or wall.

NOVEMBER

Skimmia japonica

SKIMMIA

→ Male skimmia produce attractive clusters of reddish flower buds. Female skimmia have bright red berries. Both kinds are first-rate evergreen shrubs for providing winter colour.

Skimmia japonica 'Rubella' is a compact variety that grows 30 inches (75 cm) high and has handsome red buds all winter.

S. reevesiana is a special dwarf form that grows only 18 to 24 inches (45 to 60 cm) high and is self-pollinating, which enables it to produce crimson berries without a partner.

Skimmia is sometimes prone to attack from mites, particularly when it is stressed as a result of inadequate watering or poor soil.

Grow it in the mixed shrub border where it can be easily seen in winter, along with hellebores, pink viburnum and winter-flowering camellias. Or combine it in a container with heuchera, gaultheria and ornamental grasses to create an attractive display for your front entrance over the winter.

TYPE
shrub

SIZE
*18 to 30 inches
(45 to 75 cm)*

LOCATION
shade

CONDITIONS
*well-drained, acidic but
humus-rich soil*

NOVEMBER

TYPE
shrub

SIZE
*8 to 10 feet
(2.5 to 3 m)*

LOCATION
full sun

CONDITIONS
average, well-drained soil

Taxus × media 'Hicksii'

HICK'S YEW

➔ Hedges are very important structures in the garden. They create privacy, screen the garden from cold winds and provide a solid backdrop for a herbaceous border. They can block out eyesores or provide dramatic corridors.

Yew makes the classiest hedge. It is slow-growing, which means you have to be patient, and it is more expensive than other hedging plants, but in the long run you end up with a better, more solid, elegant hedge.

Common English yew is *Taxus baccata*. Left undisturbed, it eventually grows to 40 feet (12 m) or more. However, the best kind for hedging is Hick's yew (*T. × media* 'Hicksii'), a cross between the English yew (*T. baccata*) and the Japanese yew (*T. cuspidata*).

Hick's yew produces a narrow, upright bush with dark green foliage that holds its colour. It requires minimal maintenance.

Brown's yew (*Taxus × media* 'Brownii') has more of a vase shape and is a good choice if you want a slow-growing formal hedge in a shaded area. It grows to 8 feet (2.5 m).

The golden Irish yew, *T. baccata* 'Fastigiata Aurea', is another fine hedging plant. It has golden-yellow leaves on new growth, while 'Fastigiata Aureomarginata' has more yellow than golden variegated leaves. They are all capable of growing 25 to 30 feet (7.5 to 9 m), but can be kept down through pruning.

Among the Japanese yews, *T. cuspidata* 'Nana' is low-growing and wide-spreading while 'Capitata' has a pronounced pyramidal shape. Both tolerate regular pruning, making them ideal for a hedge or topiary.

Wollemia nobilis

WOLLEMI PINE

→ The most desirable pine to have in the garden these days is the ancient Wollemi pine, a tree that dates back more than two hundred million years to the Jurassic Age and the time of the dinosaurs.

This tree was thought to be extinct—botanists knew of it only from fossils that were ninety million years old. It became the talk of the horticultural world when in 1994 a tiny grove of about one hundred trees was accidentally discovered in a deep rainforest canyon about 125 miles west of Sydney, Australia.

A relative of the Norfolk Island pine and the monkey puzzle tree, it has some curious habits. In winter, it produces a snowcone-like protective coating at the tips of branches. And, after it reaches five years old, its bark appears to turn chocolate brown. It responds aggressively to pruning by quickly producing new growth to replace any losses.

It grows quickly and tolerates temperatures from 23 to 113°F (−5 to 45°C). But, you have to remember this is a tree that has survived dozens of ice ages and all sorts of other challenges. I mean, it was around long, long before humans appeared, and it has outlived the dinosaurs and many other now-extinct species. It's a tough cookie.

TYPE
conifer

SIZE
60 to 110 feet (18 to 33 m)

LOCATION
sun to light shade

CONDITIONS
average, well-drained soil

NOVEMBER

DECEMBER

TO-DO LIST

○ *Plant paperwhite bulbs in pots for a fragrant indoor display. Simply press the bulbs into a bed of pebbles or gravel and add water until it just touches the bottom of the bulbs. Green shoots will quickly appear, followed by white flowers with a pungent aroma.*

○ Grow pre-chilled hyacinth bulbs in soil in pots, or in water in elegant forcing jars (available at garden centres). These "prepared hyacinths" have already been through a chilling process to reduce the time it takes for the bulb to bloom from 14 to 8 weeks.

○ Water plants sparingly to prevent them becoming waterlogged and succumbing to root rot.

○ Keep an eye out for whitefly and red spider mite on plants being overwintered in the greenhouse or a frost-free inside location.

○ Lime your lawn if you forgot to do this in November, and also spread some lime around the base of lilacs and over the vegetable garden. This will reduce acidity and improve soil. Lime actually acts as a fertilizer by allowing plants to better access micronutrients. You can also do this in spring.

○ Lightly prune hollies, cotoneaster and pyracantha; gather branches and berries for use in wreaths and seasonal decorations.

○ Finish garden cleanup: rake leaves, bag the mushy yellow leaves of hostas and cut down the tall leaves of crocosmia to make way for new growth in spring.

○ Order seed catalogues. New varieties are often in short supply, so it pays to get your order in early.

○ Put your feet up and take a rest. You deserve it!

DECEMBER

Betula utilis jacquemontii

HIMALAYAN BIRCH

TYPE
tree

SIZE
*35 to 40 feet
(10.5 to 12 m)*

LOCATION
full sun to part shade

CONDITIONS
*moist but well-
drained soil*

→ Wondering what kind of birch to plant? Your best choice is either the white-barked Himalayan birch (*Betula utilis jacquemontii*) or Young's weeping birch (*B. pendula* 'Youngii'), depending on how much space you have.

My pick would be the *B. jacquemontii*. This tree, which is native to northern India and the Himalayas, is as beautiful in the middle of winter with its fabulous pure white trunk and branches as it is in summer when it has all its leaves.

After 20 years it can reach incredible heights, but it always remains slender and graceful. Top cultivars are 'Silver Shadow', 'Jermyns', 'Moonbeam', 'Doorenbos' ('Snow Queen') and 'Grayswood Ghost'.

For a courtyard or small garden, however, Young's weeping birch is ideal because it's short and compact. It is usually sold as a weeping standard, grafted onto a trunk about 6 to 7 feet (1.8 to 2 m) off the ground. It soon forms an umbrella shape that can fit next to a small pond or be the centrepiece of a flower garden.

Chimonanthus praecox

WINTERSWEET

→ This native Chinese deciduous shrub is aptly named "wintersweet" as it produces cheery, sulfur-yellow flowers with purple centres in the middle of winter, sometimes as early as November.

The fragrant blooms appear on leafless branches and last for about a month if they are not damaged by rain and hard frosts. In spring, the shrub's faded blooms are replaced by new leaves on the bare branches.

Branches can also be clipped and brought indoors where the flowers are a winter treat.

Most experts recommend getting the regular species, *Chimonanthus praecox*, but the cultivar 'Grandiflorus' has been highly rated by the Royal Horticultural Society. 'Lumeau' is another popular cultivar with slightly brighter yellow flowers than the common species. It also has the typical fountain-like shape and looks best planted against a dark backdrop to emphasize the brightness of the flowers.

To add interest to the shrub in summer, it helps if you plant a herbaceous clematis close by so that it can scramble over your wintersweet with a profusion of flowers.

TYPE
shrub

SIZE
*6 to 8 feet
(1.8 to 2.5 m)*

LOCATION
full sun

CONDITIONS
average, well-drained soil

DECEMBER

TYPE
shrub

SIZE
6 feet (1.8 m)

LOCATION
full sun to part shade

CONDITIONS
moist but well-drained soil

Cornus alba 'Sibirica'

RED-TWIGGED DOGWOOD

→ In the dark days of winter, the bright red stems of deciduous shrubby dogwoods can be a heartening sight, especially when set against a snow-covered landscape.

Names can be confusing in this group of plants: *Cornus sericea* refers to the red-twig, American, Western and the Red-osier dogwood. Some taxonomists also refer to it as *C. stolonifera*.

To further complicate matters, there is *C. alba*, which also has red stems and goes by the name Siberian (or Tatarian) dogwood as well as silver-leaf, red-twig or variegated dogwood. Cultivars of *C. alba* are often listed as *C. sericea* and vice versa.

The key to keeping all red-twig dogwoods producing its bright stems in winter is to prune back the entire plant as close to the ground as possible every couple of years in early spring. This results in fresh growth of red stems.

'Sibirica', a superior cultivar of *C. alba,* has exceptionally bright red shoots in winter. Other red-stemmed dogwoods to look for include 'Baileyi', 'Isanti', 'Cardinal' and 'Elegantissima'. The latter is also very popular because of its creamy variegated white and green foliage.

'Flaviramea', the yellow-twigged dogwood, is mostly sold as a cultivar of *C. stolonifera*, although you might also might find it listed as *C. sericea*. Its bark turns yellow in winter. And *C. sanguinea* 'Midwinter Fire' offers stems with an interesting mix of red, yellow and orange.

DECEMBER

TYPE
ornamental grass

SIZE
18 inches (45 cm)

LOCATION
full sun to part sun

CONDITIONS
average, well-drained soil

Festuca glauca
BLUE FESCUE

→ In spring, you can plant this grass absolutely anywhere you like. It has great blue foliage all year long, but you will appreciate it most in winter when everything else is dead and gone and it is still holding its lovely sky-blue colour.

Festuca glauca can also be used in a lawn-replacement planting scheme with heathers and sedums. Or you can grow it all on its own in a container or even in a window box. It is that versatile.

The most popular cultivar is 'Elijah Blue', which has powdery-blue leaves and grows only 18 inches (45 cm) high. This is rated by many experts as one of the brightest and best of the blue grasses, but tests have shown that it is not always consistent. Sometimes it loses it colour and becomes tatty over a few years. 'Pepindale Blue' and 'Azurit' are two cultivars that do not lose their colour

or become dishevelled.

Every year, blue *F. glauca* needs to be raked through to remove dead foliage. It will also need a haircut in early spring to keep it neat and to promote fresh new growth. Clumps will eventually need to be replaced, but they can be pulled apart and replanted and will eventually develop into mature plants.

Another excellent blue grass, especially for use in containers, is *Elymus magellanicus* (blue wheatgrass), which has vibrant blue foliage with broader leaves than blue oat grass. It's non-invasive and grows 12 to 16 inches (30 to 40 cm) high. *Koeleria glauca* (hair grass) is another quality blue ornamental grass that many gardeners have yet to discover. It's non-invasive, forms a clump 10 to 14 inches (25 to 35 cm) high and produces sandy-coloured flower spikes that can be spectacular.

DECEMBER

Helleborus niger

CHRISTMAS ROSE

TYPE
perennial

SIZE
*10 to 16 inches
(25 to 40 cm)*

LOCATION
part sun to light shade

CONDITIONS
average, well-drained soil

→ *Helleborus niger* is known as the Christmas rose, but few cultivars actually flower in time for the festive season.

'Praecox' is the exception, often flowering weeks before Christmas and continuing over the holiday period, when it consistently produces graceful nodding flowers that are white and cup-shaped. It is a cultivar that has been popular with European gardeners for many years.

Other talked-about hybrids include 'Potter's Wheel', 'White Magic', 'Eva' and 'Higham's Variety', most of which bloom from January into February. They grow 18 to 24 inches (45 to 60 cm) high.

Increasingly popular are a new group of hybrids produced by crossing *H. niger* with *H. argutifolius*. These are being sold as *H. × nigercors*. Named cultivars include 'Green Heron', 'White Beauty', 'Honeyhill Joy' and the most popular of them all, 'Ivory Prince'.

In a container, *H. niger* can be mixed with heuchera, skimmia, gaultheria and ornamental grasses. Place it close to an entrance where its delicate white buds, followed by white flowers, can be enjoyed more conveniently.

The whole hellebore group of plants is well worth getting to know, especially the later-flowering and most popular of all—the Lenten rose (*H. orientalis,* page 49).

Ilex crenata

JAPANESE HOLLY

→ A good alternative to boxwood, Japanese holly offers the added bonus of attractive blackberries in fall and winter. This shrub is a member of the holly family.

It can be clipped into a formal-looking waist-high barrier or allowed to grow to 6 feet (1.8 m) and higher.

It is also an excellent plant to use in a winter container: use it as a central "anchor plant" and surround it with heuchera to provide a splash of colour from November to February.

Top cultivars of *Ilex crenata* are 'Helleri', 'Convexa', 'Mariesii', 'Rotundifolia' and 'Hetzii', the last of which is a dwarf form that grows only 2 feet (60 cm) high.

Also look for 'Sky Pencil', which is a unique columnar form that grows only 45 cm wide but can eventually reach 10 feet (3 m), and 'Lemon Gem', which has lime-green foliage.

TYPE *shrub*

SIZE *6 feet (1.8 m)*

LOCATION *full sun to part shade*

CONDITIONS *average, well-drained soil*

Lonicera nitida 'Baggesen's Gold'

SHRUBBY HONEYSUCKLE, BOXLEAF HONEYSUCKLE

→ It is the bright tiny yellow leaves of 'Baggesen's Gold' that make it so desirable as a contrast foliage plant and as a general brightener of the garden.

Shrubby honeysuckles have long been appreciated for their usefulness in the shrub border or for creating low, informal hedges. They can also be grown as a feature in a container.

'Baggesen's Gold', which is also known as the "boxleaf honeysuckle," needs protection from the afternoon sun in summer or its leaves will scorch.

Other first-rate yellow-foliage plants to consider include the golden elderberry (*Sambucus racemosa* 'Sutherland Gold'), *Cotinus coggygria* 'Golden Spirit', *Choisya ternata* 'Sundance', *Spiraea* × 'Gold Mound', *Philadelphus coronarius* 'Aureus' and *Physocarpus opulifolius* 'Dart's Gold'. These are all great for injecting light and striking texture to the garden.

TYPE *shrub*

SIZE *4 to 6 feet (1.2 to 1.8 m)*

LOCATION *full sun to part shade*

CONDITIONS *moist but well-drained soil*

DECEMBER

TYPE
conifer

SIZE
4 feet (1.2 m)

LOCATION
full sun to light shade

CONDITIONS
well-drained soil

Pinus mugo

MUGO PINE

→ One of the most common evergreens used in low-maintenance schemes, the mugo (or mugho) pine is a solid, meat-and-potatoes type of low-maintenance landscape plant that provides structure and evergreen colour year round.

It is highly disease resistant, drought tolerant and slow-growing.

Also consider the dwarf mugo pine (*Pinus mugo* 'Pumilio'), which is very drought tolerant and even a little shade tolerant; 'Mops', which has an attractive globe shape as well as brown buds in winter; and 'Gnom', which is the most compact, growing only 15 inches (38 cm) high after 20 years.

The dwarf blue Scotch pine (*P. sylvestris* 'Glauca Nana') is related to the mugo pine and grows slowly to an ultimate height of 5 to 8 feet (1.5 to 2.5 m).

Dwarf conifers can give a garden the feeling of structural integrity and permanence. Here are some other great picks, all cultivars of *Thujas occidentalis:*

- 'Danica' has dark green foliage, turns blue-green in winter and grows to 30 inches (75 cm).
- 'Rheingold' is conical-shaped with golden-yellow foliage and grows 3 to 5 feet (90 cm to 1.5 m).
- 'Aurea Nana' has golden-yellow foliage and grows only 3 feet (90 cm) high.
- 'Little Gem' has a pyramidal shape and emerald-green foliage. It grows 12 to 15 inches (30 to 38 cm) high, making it an excellent plant for a planter on a patio.
- 'Little Giant' is a stocky shrub that keeps its bright green look in winter and grows to 40 inches (1 m).

DECEMBER

Viburnum × bodnantense 'Dawn'

PINK VIBURNUM

→ One of the true stars of the winter garden, this pink-flowering viburnum is a deciduous shrub that produces clusters of extremely fragrant, tubular pink flowers from December through to early spring.

Hardy to Zone 6, pink viburnum's flowers are indifferent to frosts, managing to hold their colour and form even on the coldest days in January.

It once was known as 'Pink Dawn', but now seems to be more widely referred to by nurseries as simply 'Dawn'. The word *bodnantense* refers to Bodnant Gardens, North Wales, where the hybrid was raised in 1935.

Pink viburnum should be lightly pruned in March or April every year to prevent it from looking wild and unkempt. First remove dead, damaged, crossing or diseased branches, and then snip judiciously to enhance the overall shape of the shrub.

It is best placed in a spot where it can be easily seen throughout the winter, but also where the heavy scent of the flowers can be appreciated. Its only rival in the winter garden is witch hazel (*Hamamelis mollis*, page 13), which also produces sensational fragrant flowers.

TYPE
shrub

SIZE
10 to 15 feet
(3 to 4.5 m)

LOCATION
full sun to part shade

CONDITIONS
average, well-drained soil

DECEMBER

Index

Photo Credits

WE ARE GRATEFUL FOR PHOTOGRAPHS SUPPLIED BY THE FOLLOWING:

Walter Altenmueller,
Reimer's Nursery
Yarrow

Clearview Horticultural
Aldergrove

Hawaiian Botanicals
and Water Gardens
Richmond

Heather Johnson
North Vancouver

Heritage Perennials
Abbotsford

Netherlands Flower Bulb
Information Center (NFBIC)
www.bulbpix.com

Pan American Nursery
Surrey

Phoenix Perennials
Richmond

Rhododendron Species Foundation
Federal Way, WA

Rob Silins
Nanaimo

Select Roses
Langley

Skagit Gardens
Mount Vernon, WA

University of BC Botanical Garden
Vancouver

The Vancouver Sun

Van Belle Nursery Inc.
Abbotsford

Antonie van den Bos
www.botanypictures.com

Van Noort Bulb Company
Langley